Dirty Jokes in a Dinner Jacket

After-dinner Stories for Speakers

Dirty Jokes in a Dinner Jacket

After-dinner Stories for Speakers

The Laughter Lines Team

Compiled by Ken Morgan

foulsham

LONDON • NEW YORK • TORONTO • SYDNEY

foulsham

The Publishing House, Bennetts Close,
Cippenham, Slough, Berkshire, SL1 5AP, England

ISBN 0-572-02490-8

Printed in Great Britain by St. Edmundsbury Press, Bury St. Edmunds, Suffolk.

Contents

Introduction

These stories, anecdotes and jokes speak for themselves. They have been collected together from a variety of highly amusing and witty sources, to give you some seriously funny material for your after-dinner entertainment. They are on all kinds of topics – from sex to animals (and sometimes sex and animals) – and, for those times when you want to find a favourite joke again, or choose something on a specific topic, there's a comprehensive index to help you.

Whenever you decide to use a humorous story in your after-dinner speech, make sure you practise and personalise it as much as you can. Your own additions, embellishments, gestures and presentation will make all the difference. There is nothing worse than hearing someone 'read out' a joke from a book! And whether you're telling a lengthy shaggy dog story or a zippy one-liner, never forget the crucial factor: timing. Make sure you know exactly where to pause, where to place the emphasis and when to take a deep breath while the audience react, so that you deliver the final punchline at exactly the right moment. The best way to work this out is to tell the joke to some friends and pay close attention to how they respond.

Enjoy the collection; hopefully it will provide you with a vast storehouse of humour to pep up your speech and amuse your guests.

Trust Me, I'm a Doctor

Mirth occasioned by the medical profession

An American girl goes to see the doctor and says, 'Doctor, doctor, I've got trouble.'

He says, 'What's that, honey?'

'Well,' she says, 'I've got this letter C on my chest,' and she takes off her shirt and shows him this great big C like a tattoo on her chest. 'I've got this boyfriend and he's at California University and when he comes home on vacation he's so impatient to get into bed with me and do it that he just can't wait to get his T-shirt off, so we get hot and sweaty and the C printed on my chest is off his T-shirt.'

'Honey, don't worry about a thing,' says the doctor. 'I'll get some white spirit and I'll soon move that for you.' He does this and off it comes.

A couple of weeks later another girl comes in and says, 'Doctor, doctor, I've got this terrible problem. I'll take my T-shirt off to show you. I've got this O on my chest. It's my boyfriend. He's at Ohio University and when he comes home on vacation he's so impatient for sex he can't wait to get his T-shirt off. We get all hot and sweaty and it's given me this O on my chest.'

'Honey,' says the doctor, 'I just had a similar case two weeks ago and I'll soon fix you up with some white spirit,' and he rubs it and the mark comes off.

Two weeks later the doctor gets another girl in and she's got this big M on her chest. She says, 'Doctor, doctor, I've got this terrible trouble on my chest.'

She takes off her T-shirt, but before she can say anything else the doctor says, 'Okay, honey, I know what it is. When your boyfriend comes home from university, he's so impatient for sex, he can't wait to get his shirt off and you're all naked, hot and sweaty and you get that mark on your chest.'

The girl says, 'That's right doctor, that's right.'

He says, 'And I'll tell you something else: he's at Michigan University.'

'Oh no,' she says, 'He's at Wichita.'

A doctor says to his patient, 'I'm terribly sorry, old chap, but we've established what's wrong with you. You've got a very severe case of GASH.'

'What the hell's GASH?'

'Well, it's a combination of gonorrhoea, AIDS, syphilis and herpes.'

'Good God, what on earth can you do for me?'

'We're going to put you into a special single room with the doors and windows locked, barred and bolted, and we are going to feed you on pizza and pancakes.'

'Why pizza and pancakes?'

'Those are the only things we can get under the door.'

There are three surgeons discussing which occupation provides the easiest patients to work on. One of them says, 'I like operating on airline pilots because when you open them up, there's always a checklist there.'

The second one says, 'I prefer electricians because they're colour-coded, so it's blue to blue, brown to brown, and so on when you're putting them back together again.'

The third one says, 'I prefer bankers: they're definitely the easiest because they've only got two parts – the arsehole and the mouth – and they're interchangeable.'

A chap has consulted his doctor and the doctor asks him, 'What's your sex life like?'

'It's not bad.'

So the doctor asks, 'How often do you make love? Tell me about it.'

'Well,' he replies, 'I make love to the wife about seven times a week. Of course, I've got a lovely secretary and I make love to her once a day. Plus I masturbate every morning and have wet dreams every night.'

'That's terribly interesting,' says the doctor. 'Tell me, which do you prefer?'

'Oh, the wet dreams,' replies the man.

'Why's that?' asks the doctor.

'You meet a better class of woman.'

A bloke walks into a doctor's surgery and the doctor says, 'What's wrong?'

The man says, 'I've got a cricket ball stuck up my arse.'

And the doctor says, 'How's that?' (Howsatt?)

A guy goes to the doctor for an insurance medical and before he starts to examine him, the doctor says, 'Look, would you mind indulging me, I've got a little hobby – guessing people's ages. I've become extremely expert at it and I want to have a guess at yours before I look at the insurance papers. Do you mind if I have a go?'

The guy says, 'No, you can try if you like.'

'All right,' says the doctor and looks at him, examines him, sounds his heart and says, 'You're 57 years and 5 months of age.'

The guy says, 'You're horribly wrong! I'm 75.'

'I don't believe it,' replies the doctor. 'You can't be, I couldn't be that wrong.'

'Well,' says the patient, 'look at the insurance papers.'

The doctor looks at them and says, 'My God, you are 75! What an incredible mistake, I've never been more wrong in my life; I wouldn't have believed it. So tell me, how old was your father when he died?'

'Oh,' came the reply, 'he's still alive.'

'Well, how old is he?'

'He's 94.'

'94? He's in a bit of a state then, isn't he?'

'Oh no, he goes jogging every day, cuts logs, swims, plays football, the lot. He's incredibly fit,' says the man.

'Good God, how old was your grandfather when he died?' the doctor asks.

'He's alive, too. He's 118 and he got married last week.'

'Whatever makes a bloke that age want to get married again?' the doctor asks.

'Who said he *wanted* to get married?'

A woman rings the doctor's surgery and says, 'Doctor, doctor, come quickly! The baby's swallowed a condom.'

The doctor says, 'Well, I've just got a patient with me but I'll clear her soon and I'll be over in about ten minutes if you can just hang on.'

In five minutes, the phone rings again and the same lady comes on the phone and says, 'Don't bother, doctor, we've found another one.'

The advantage of being a consultant is that he's the only man who can ask a beautiful young woman he's never met to take off all her clothes, touch her in the most intimate places, and then demand a fee from her husband.

There are two black African doctors in Cape Town and one says to the other, 'You know that white guy in ward 14. Have you told him he's going to die?'

'Yes.'

'You bastard, I wanted to tell him myself.'

'I know who you are,' said the doctor to his patient. 'You're the chap who had the arse transplant and it rejected you.'

A psychiatrist says to his patient, 'What appears to be the problem, Mr Jones?'

'I can't get on with anybody, fat arse.'

A man goes to the doctor complaining about a rash on his chest. The doctor tells him to strip off, looks at him and says, 'Good Lord, isn't that incredible! I've never seen a white man with brown balls.'

The patient gets very excited and shouts, 'Mind your own bloody business about my brown balls. I've come to see you about the rash on my chest.'

The doctor looks at the rash on his chest and says, 'Ah, I think I know what it is. Do you wear a string vest?'

'Yes I do,' replies the man.

The doctor says, 'Well, your wife isn't washing your clothes properly. She's using rather strong detergent but she's not rinsing it out of your vest thoroughly and it's irritating your skin.'

The man goes home and he gets hold of his wife and says, 'You lazy bitch, you lazy 'orrible bitch. I've been to the doctor because I've had all this trouble with the rash on my chest and he tells me it's because you're too bloody idle to wash my vests out properly so I've been suffering from this rash on my chest all this time.'

'Don't you talk to me about being lazy,' she snaps back. 'You've given me eight children but you never give me enough money to look after the house or them. I work my fingers to the bone 22 hours a day looking after you and all the kids and going to work and everything. God, I don't even have time to wipe my arse.'

He says, 'And that's another thing.'

A doctor says to his patient, 'I've got good and bad news, I'm afraid. The bad news is that we have decided you're definitely homosexual. The good news is that I love you, darling.'

A fella walks into the Nuffield Hospital reception area and asks the receptionist if he can talk to one of the surgeons.

'That's a bit unusual, sir,' she says, 'but I'll see if anyone is free to see you.' She leaves the desk and when she comes back she says, 'Mr Black will be able to spare you a few minutes. He'll be down directly.'

When the surgeon arrives, he says, 'Yes, sir, what can I do for you?'

'I'd like a quotation for a piles operation, please,' says the man.

'Piles operation quotation? That's unusual, but yes, I think we can do that. Let me think. It would be about £2,000 give or take a pound or two.'

'What, £2,000? That seems an enormous sum of money for a simple operation like piles. How do you get to such a large sum of money?'

'Well, it's £600 for three days and nights in the Nuffield.'

'What do you mean, three days and nights in the Nuffield, what's that about?'

'Well, after the operation, the patient has to recuperate for three days and our standard charge at the Nuffield is £200 a day.'

'I don't want any of that nonsense. Goodness gracious me, just pampering, that is. In, operation, and home again same day. Can we now reduce it by £600, your estimate?'

'Yes, I suppose so, it's possible. It's not advisable, of course, but yes, that can happen, you can go home the same day.'

'Okay, that's it then, we're at £1,400 now. How did we get to £1,400?'

'It's £400 for your anaesthetist.'

'What's an anaesthetist?'

'He's the chap who renders the patients unconscious while performing the operation so they don't feel any pain while I'm cutting them about a bit. He gives them an anaesthetic.'

'Oh, we don't need any kind of that nonsense – tremendous tolerance to pain. No problem at all with pain. Look, this is what we're going to do: in, operation, home again same day, no anaesthetic, so are we talking about £1,000 now?'

'Yes, I suppose we are.'

'How do you get to £1,000, may I ask? It still seems a lot of money.'

'Well, there's £200 for the theatre nurses.'

'Theatre nurses, what do they do?'

'They pass me the correct knives and scalpels and sutures at the right moment when I'm performing the operation.'

'How many times have you done this operation?'

'Oh, hundreds and hundreds of times, if not thousands.'

'Surely to God you know which knife and fork to use by now if you've done it hundreds and hundreds of times? Surely you don't need any slips of girls passing you the implements at the appropriate time? Surely you can do it by yourself?'

'Well, I suppose I could really. Yes, I can, okay.'

'So what are we now? £800?'

'Yes.'

'What's that for?'

'That's for me doing the operation.'

'What? How long does it take you?'

'About half an hour.'

'Good God! £800 for half an hour, that's immoral, it's indecent. £800 for half an hour! It's absolutely ridiculous. I'm not giving you that. Look, I'll give you £400 in notes.'

So the surgeon thinks long and hard and he says, 'Can you make it five?

'All right then, £500 in notes, when can you do it?'

'A week on Wednesday.'

'Fine, I'll bring her in about half past nine.'

A sign on the wall of a maternity ward said: 'Remember, the first 10 minutes of life are the most dangerous.'

To which someone had added, scrawled underneath in felt pen: 'And the last 10 minutes aren't so bloody clever either.'

Two Pakistani doctors are arguing in a hospital corridor.

One of them says, 'I think you spell it w-h-o-m-b-e.'

And the other one says, 'No, no, no, you definitely spell it w-h-o-o-m-e.'

The matron's just walking past and she hears the conversation and says, 'I'm sorry, gentlemen, but you're both wrong, you spell it w-o-m-b.'

When she's gone away one of them turns to the other and says, 'Stupid bitch. I bet she's never even heard a buffalo fart under water.'

'I was rushed into the premature ejaculation ward last Friday.

'It was touch and go.

'I discharged myself on Monday.'

After the micro-surgeons' conference in New York, the leading surgeons were in the bar and, being drunk as skunks, began to reminisce over their greatest feats.

The first, an Australian surgeon, explained, 'We had a chap caught in a printing press at a factory last year and all that was left of him was his little finger. Our team of surgeons constructed a new hand and built a new arm, engineered a new body and ultimately, when he returned to the workforce, he was so efficient, he put five men out of work.'

'That's nothing,' said the American surgeon. 'We had a worker trapped inside a nuclear reactor and all that was left of him was his hair. We constructed a new skull, a new torso and new limbs and returned him to the workforce. He's so efficient now, he's put 50 men out of work.'

The English surgeon was not to be outdone. 'I was walking down the street when I got the smell of a fart. So I took it back to the hospital in a garbage bag, let it loose on the table and we got to work. First of all we wrapped an arsehole around it, built a bum around that, attached a body to one end and legs to the other. Gradually it turned into the chancellor of the exchequer *(use the current name)* and he has put the whole fucking country out of work.'

A royal visitor to a hospital ward is going down the ward with the matron, and there's a man lying in bed masturbating.

The royal visitor says, 'What's that man doing there?'

'Oh, Your Highness, he's going to have a vasectomy and we need a sample of his semen for that.'

They walk a little further and there's another man with a nurse bending over him giving him a blow job. The royal visitor says, 'What's happening there?'

So the matron says, 'Well, he's having a vasectomy too, but he's with BUPA.'

A chemist is interviewing a 16-year-old lad to be his assistant.

'Ooh,' he tells him, 'I do like you, you're a lovely boy and I think you're absolutely super. You've come flying through all the exams and tests so far to be my personal assistant, and as far as I'm concerned you've got the job now. But one thing you've still got to do is to pass a very important smell test. It's essential for a chemist's assistant to have an exceptionally accurate sense of smell. So, what I want to do is blindfold you and I'm going to give you three different things to smell. If you get them right, you've got the job. Do you mind being blindfolded?'

'No, sir.'

'Right, I'll put the blindfold on,' the chemist says. 'First thing, have a good smell at this. What is it?'

'It's TCP, sir.'

'Exactly right,' says the chemist, 'and you're so quick, I think that's wonderful, I do hope you get the next two right, then you can work for me – and I want you to work for me very, very much. I think you're a lovely boy,' he says as he gives the next thing to the boy to smell. 'What's that?'

'Glycerin euthymol, sir,' comes the answer.

'Oh, that was a difficult one,' says the chemist. 'That's harder than TCP and you've got it right ever so quick again. You're nearly there. One more and you've got the job. Now have a good smell at this.'

The lad gives a good, long sniff and passes out on the spot. He stays unconscious for half an hour. When he eventually comes round, he says, 'God, what was that?'

The chemist says, 'Chloroform – doesn't it make your bum sore?'

A man goes into a chemist shop and says, 'A packet of French letters please.'

The young girl assistant says, 'What are French letters?'

The customer replies, 'They're those things that a man puts on his personal parts to stop making babies and catching diseases and things.'

'Oh,' she replies, 'you mean condoms.'

'Is that what they call them now? – I haven't bought them for 25 years or so. It's only this AIDS thing that has made me think about it now in case I catch anything.'

'Yes, we call them condoms now,' she says. 'What size do you take, sir?'

'Size?' he says. 'I thought they were all the same size.'

'Well, maybe they were when you were buying French letters,' she replies, 'but we're much more sophisticated now and we have different sizes.'

'I haven't got a clue what size I take,' says the customer, 'they were all the same size when I was buying them.'

'Well, we know about people like you,' replies the assistant, 'and we have a little fitting room specially for you. I'll take you there.'

So she takes him to the fitting room and says, 'There you are, sir, you can draw a curtain behind you. On the side there you'll find a testing board. Try the testing board and come back and tell me in a moment what size you take and I'll supply you.'

The man looks at the testing board, and it's a board about a foot square and an inch thick and there's a piece of sorbo rubber 10 inches thick stuck on to it. Drilled in the sorbo rubber are ten different-sized holes numbered one to ten.

Ten minutes later he goes back to the young lady assistant, looking a bit flushed. 'Right, sir,' she says, 'what size do you take?'

'Oh bugger the condoms,' he says, 'how much do you want for the fitting board?'

Trust Me, I'm a Builder!

Wit occasioned by the working man

A crane driver is sitting on the top of his tower crane in his little cab and suddenly a 16-year-old lad appears, and he's climbed up the ladder all the way from the ground. So the driver says, 'Who the hell are you, what are you doing?'

'I'm a youth training assistant for you. I've got to learn the trade of driving the tower crane and you've got to teach me.'

'Oh that's great, I'm delighted, especially as you've come up just now.'

'Why?'

'Because I'm dying for a pee, and I'm very visible in the cab here, so normally I have to climb all the way down the tower crane to the ground and go to the toilet on the site, but now I've got you to help, there's a spot out on the jib arm where I can actually be hidden, and I can have a pee from there which'll save me climbing all the way down.'

'How do you get out on to the jib?'

'I can go out in the bucket. You can operate it, and I'll show you what to do. There's two levers, one's got an arrow forward and one's got an arrow back. To send the bucket out, just push the lever forward and it'll keep going forward till I shout to you to stop it. Put the lever into neutral, then I'll shout again to you to bring me back again using the other lever, after I've had a pee.'

'What's this red button for?' asks the lad.

'For God's sake don't touch that, that's the button that opens the bucket doors! Leave that well alone! Have you got that clear?'

'Yes I have, I've got it all clear. No worries.'

So the crane driver gets into the bucket and says, 'Right, off we go.' The trainee pushes the lever forward where the arrow's pointing and the guy in the bucket goes out along the arm of the crane, and when he gets halfway along, where he's hidden from view, he shouts, 'Stop'. After a while he shouts, 'Back'. But this takes the trainee by surprise and makes him jump! His hand shakes and he hits the red button by mistake and the crane driver drops out of the bucket 300 feet to his death down below.

At the inquest, the coroner's asking the witnesses what they knew about this tragic accident. One of them is an Irish labourer and the coroner says to him, 'Paddy, what do you know about this tragic accident?'

And Paddy says to him, 'Well, I do know one thing, sir, I think he was a sex maniac.'

The coroner says, 'What makes you think that?'

'Well, I was working on the tenth floor of this building when the crane driver fell past me, and as he fell past me to his death, he was holding his dick in one hand and shouting at the top of his voice, "C-U-N-T!".'

A plumber is called to a house to do a very simple job. He's there about 10 minutes and the housewife says, 'How much do I owe you?'

So he says, 'That'll be £40.'

The women is horrified. '*How* much?' she says. 'My doctor only charges me £20.'

And the plumber says, 'I know, I only charged £20 when I practised as a doctor.'

A blind man applies for a job in a timber yard, but the foreman tells him he can't employ him because he's blind.

'Never mind about me being blind, I've forgotten more about wood than you'll ever know. I've been in the game for years.'

The foreman says, 'Well, if you can't see, you won't be able to tell one kind of wood from another.'

'I would,' he says. 'I can tell it by the smell – try me.'

So the foreman gets a bit of wood and asks him what it is.

'By the smell, that's mahogany from Africa.'

'Blimey, you're right,' says the foreman. So he gets another piece of wood and says, 'What's that?'

The blind man says, 'That's teak from the Far East.'

Impressed, the foreman gets a third piece of wood and says, 'What's that then?'

'That's English oak from the New Forest.'

'Right again!' says the foreman. By now, the foreman is getting a bit hacked off because the blind man is so clever, so he gets a small piece of timber from a kipper box and he rubs it round his secretary's panties and pushes it under the blind man's nose. 'What's that?' he asks.

The blind man says, 'Ah, you can't fool me, that's a piece of a shithouse door from Grimsby.'

A girl gets into a taxi and says, 'Take me to the station.'

The taxi driver takes her to the station and says, 'Right, miss, that'll be £3.50.'

She says, 'I haven't got any money but I'll pay you another way – turn around and look.' She pulls her skirt right up and she's not wearing any knickers. 'Will you take it out of this?' she says, pointing at her fanny.

'Haven't you got anything smaller?' asks the taxi driver.

Two Irish navvies are sitting on a train and when the train stops at the station another chap gets in. One of the men says to his pal, 'Look who that is who's just got into the train: that's the Archbishop of Canterbury.'

His pal says, 'Don't be silly, that isn't the Archbishop of Canterbury! He wouldn't be travelling with us in a second-class compartment, he'd be in his Rolls going up the M1.'

'I tell you, it's the Archbishop of Canterbury,' says the first man. 'In fact, I'll bet you £5 it's the Archbishop of Canterbury.'

'You're on,' says his mate. 'Here's my fiver, I'll go and ask him,' and he walks across to this chap and says, 'Excuse me, but aren't you the Archbishop of Canterbury?'

The bloke says, 'Mind your own fucking business.' So the man goes back to his pal and says, 'Sorry, mate, the bet's off.'

'Why's that?'

'He wouldn't tell us.'

A girl with no arms and no legs is lying on the beach stark naked. The guy picking up litter on the beach decides to stop and chat to her. So he strolls up to her and says, 'You're a very attractive girl, have you ever been kissed?'

'No,' she says, so he kisses her.

He says, 'Have you ever had your tits fondled?'

'No,' she says, so he fondles her tits.

Then he says, 'Have you ever been fucked?'

'No,' she says.

'You soon will be,' he says, 'the tide's coming in.'

Three builders are swapping stories about memory and how far back they can remember.

One chap says, 'I can remember when I was six months old because I can remember sitting in my pram and we must have been outside the butcher's shop 'cos this fella with a blue and white striped apron and a straw hat came out and was talking to my mother, and I can hear him saying now, "What a lovely little boy, Mrs Smith, how old is he?", and I can remember my mother saying, "He's six months old today."'

The next chap says, 'I can beat you easily on that. In fact, I can beat everybody. My first memory is of opening my eyes and seeing a fellow with a funny white mask covering half his face and this thing, it must have been a stethoscope, hanging round his neck and I'm looking at him upside-down. Then I remember feeling a stinging pain in my arse as this fella smacks me and I hear him saying to my mother, "It's all right, Mrs Jones. You have a beautiful, perfect, bouncing baby boy." That was the minute I was born.'

The third man says, 'I can beat both of you. I can remember going to a party with my father and coming home with my mother.'

One builder says to another, 'Would you like a bit of cunt?'

And his mate says, 'Why, are you breaking one up?'

'Good God, look at your stomach, Jack! If that had been on a woman I'd say she was pregnant.'

'It has been, and she is.'

A young lad of 16 takes a job in a men's and women's outfitters and he goes to the boss one day about a week after he's started there and says, 'Boss, what I should do? There's a woman in here wants a trouser suit tailoring. How do I take her measurements?'

'How do you think?' says the boss. 'You use the tape measure.'

'Yes, I can do most of it, but what about the inside leg measurement?'

'Oh,' says the boss, 'that's easy. What you have to do is get a broomstick and stuff it up as far as it will go. Then add two inches for the turn-ups, subtract the wet from the dry and you've got the inside leg measurement.'

A chap was talking to his friend, who was a renowned flasher.

'Didn't I hear you were retired?' he says.

'No, I'm sticking it out for another 12 months.'

'This is Liverpool tower calling Aer Lingus Flight 34A. Are you receiving me?'

'This is Aer Lingus Flight 34A receiving Liverpool tower, loud and clear.'

'Liverpool tower calling Aer Lingus Flight 34A. Could you give me your height and position please?'

'Aer Lingus flight 34A calling Liverpool tower. I'm five foot five, and I'm sitting up here in the front somewhere.'

Let's Get Down to Business

Stories and jokes from the world of work

A businessman is lying in bed in the morning in his hotel and the chambermaid knocks on the door and comes in with a tray full of cups, saucers and a teapot. She puts them down on the side, walks across to his bed, pulls the sheets back, pulls his dick out of his pyjamas and gives him a blow job. When it's all over, he says, 'Well, thanks very much, what was that all about?'

She says, 'I'm the Goblin Teasmaid.'

The members of the executive board are all sitting round the table in the boardroom, with the chairman at the head of the table.

'Right, gentlemen,' says the chairman. 'The first item on the agenda is to ask you which one of you has not fucked my secretary.'

There's a long silence and eventually one guy holds up a quivering hand. So the chairman says, 'That's settled, then. You go out and sack her.'

A businessman is interviewing an attractive young girl for a job.

'Well, you look pretty good to me,' he tells her, 'and you sound very efficient. In fact, there are two jobs available here: one is as my personal secretary and the other is as the telephonist/receptionist. You can have either job as far as I'm concerned. Which one would you prefer?'

'What are the differences between the two?' she asks.

'Well,' the man replies, 'The obvious difference is the type of work, but there's also a big difference in pay – as my secretary you get £6 an hour and as the receptionist you only get £3 an hour. There is one other difference – I'm a very virile chap and I sometimes get the urge in the office – I just can't help it, it's one of those things. As my secretary, you're expected to make yourself available to me in the widest sense of the word.'

So the girl says, 'Well, you're not too old and you're not too bad looking and £6 an hour is £6 an hour. I'll take the job as secretary.'

'Right,' he says, 'you can start at 9 o'clock on Monday morning.'

The following Monday morning, he arrives at ten past nine and the girl is sitting at the typewriter.

'Right,' he says 'I feel like it. Get 'em off and get on the couch,' and he has his wicked way with her on the couch. When it's all over she sits up and says,

'My God, you don't waste much time do you?'

And he replies, 'I don't waste much money either, you're fired.'

A very sharp businessman is sitting next to an attractive woman on a transatlantic flight to New York. Never one to miss an opportunity, he decides to chat her up.

'Hi there,' he says. 'Since we shall be travelling together, perhaps we should introduce ourselves. What's your name?'

'Hello,' says the woman. 'People call me Nan.'

'That's an unusual name,' he says. 'Why do they call you that?'

'Because I'm the president of the National Association of Nymphomaniacs.'

'How very interesting! That's incredible, is there anything particular that you are into as the president of that?'

'Yes! I'm crazy about American Indians and Jews. If you would like to call on me, I'll give you my telephone number and address in New York.'

So he says, 'That'll be fine.'

And she says, 'Who shall I expect to call?

And he says, 'Tonto Cohen.'

'I had your secretary on the telephone this morning.'

'That's funny, I can't even get her on the desk.'

Two blokes are sitting at the office Christmas dinner. During the after–dinner speeches, one of them turns to the other and whispers, 'Why aren't you laughing at the speaker?'

And his colleague says, 'He said I hadn't earned my Christmas bonus so I'm not letting him know he's funny. I'm going to wait till I get home to laugh.'

There's a typical commuter train which runs every morning at 7.30 from Surbiton up to Waterloo in London and, as is normal with these things, the same eight blokes are in the compartment every morning. They never speak, they never converse, they just sit behind their *Telegraph* or their *Times* newspapers and off they go up to London to their daily jobs.

Then one of them retires and his place is taken by another chap, like all the others, dressed in typical bowler hat, striped trousers, with rolled umbrella. He sits there and again he doesn't say a word, but they are intrigued by one particular difference with him. Every morning when they're about five minutes out of Surbiton, he takes his wallet out from his inside pocket, opens it, takes out a folded piece of paper, opens out the paper, puts it to his nose, has a little sniff, seems to enjoy it very much, and then carefully folds the paper up, puts it in his wallet, and back in his pocket again.

This goes on for some six months. Of course, they're all very curious about what he's doing but, in typical English fashion, they don't speak, until after about six months one of them can't stand it any more and he says to this chap just after he's taken his wallet out of his pocket, 'Excuse me, sir, but I am most intrigued by your performance every morning with your wallet and little folded bit of paper. I know it's frightfully rude of me as we haven't been introduced, but may I ask you, sir, what it is that you take out of your wallet and sniff, which seems to please you so very much?'

The guy with the wallet, who turns out not to be English but French, says, 'Monsieur, I must tell you that I am very newly married and I have a beautiful young wife with whom I am very much in love. I miss her during the daytime when I am in my office in London, so each morning as I leave the bed and she is lying there, I pluck some hairs from her fanny and fold them in the paper. From time to time during the day, I sniff the hairs and it reminds me of her, and I don't miss her quite so much.'

'What a wonderful idea,' says the Englishman. 'As a matter of fact I'm newly married myself and I miss my wife because I love her very much too. I'm going to try that – I'm going to start tomorrow.'

So the next day they're on the train and before the Frenchman starts, the Englishman takes out his wallet, opens the piece of folded paper, has a little sniff at it and has a fit of coughing.

The Frenchman says to him, 'Monsieur, do you have some problem with this?' and the Englishman says, 'Yes, I don't know why, I can't understand it. There's something not quite right.'

'Monsieur, may I try your sample to see what is wrong?'

'That's very kind of you. I would appreciate that very much,' says the Englishmen. So the Frenchman takes the Englishman's folded piece of paper, has a sniff at it and he too starts coughing. The Englishman says to him, 'Have you any idea of what is wrong?'

'Oh yes, Monsieur. I can tell you because I have been doing this for a long time. This is quite charming, but a little too near the arsehole.'

A Customer's Guide to Insurance

There was a very cautious man who never romped or played;

He never smoked, he never drank, nor ever kissed a maid.

So when he passed away, they say, insurance was denied;

For since he never lived, they claimed he never died.

A commercial traveller representing a company that makes gentlemen's underwear calls on a retailer who is always giving him a bad time, treating him like dirt.

'Yes, what do you want?' says the retailer.

'Please, sir,' says the rep, 'I've got a very good line in gentlemen's underpants.'

'Yes, suppose you have. I bet they're too pricey and not good enough quality again, like I've always been buying from you. Show me them.' So the rep shows him this pair of the underpants.

'Yes, how much are those? Too pricey, I expect.'

'Well, as a matter of fact, sir, they are on special offer and they are only 25p a pair!'

'What? 25p a pair! That's fantastic. I'll take two hundred of them right away. Can I have the vests to match?'

'Well, I'd better show you the vest first.'

'Yes, all right, let me see the vest.'

'Here's a sample vest, sir.'

'How much are those?'

'They're £10 per vest, sir.'

'What? £10 for the vest and 25p for the pants? You must be out of your mind.'

'Well now, sir, I'm not actually, as a matter of fact. I've been calling on you for something like 20 years now and I'm retiring today and you've always treated me like a piece of dog shit when I've called on you. I thought for my last visit if I could get my pants low enough and my vests high enough, you could kiss my arse. Good morning.'

An incredibly wealthy Arab from the Gulf who had money beyond the dreams of avarice – beyond your and my imagination – had five sons whom he adored. He converted to Christianity and wanted to give them all suitable Christmas presents. So he said to his eldest son, 'What would you like for a Christmas present?'

And his son said, 'Dad, I'd like a boat.' So he bought him the *QE2* from Cunard.

Then the Arab said to his second son, 'What would you like for Christmas, son?'

And his second son said, 'I would like an aeroplane, Dad,' so he bought him a Concorde from British Airways.

Then he said to the next son, 'What would you like?'

And the next son said, 'I'd like some golf clubs,' so he bought him Wentworth and Sunningdale.

Then the Arab said to the fourth son, 'Son, what would you like for Christmas?

And he said, 'Dad, I'd like a music centre.' So he bought him the Albert Hall.

Finally, he turned to his fifth and youngest son and said, 'My son, what would you like for Christmas?'

And his youngest son said, 'Dad, I'd like a cowboy outfit.' So he bought him *(name anybody's business you want to take the mickey out of)*.

A salesman for a company selling scales calls on a farmer who is out with the sheep.

'What do you want?' asks the farmer.

'I'm from Acme Scales, sir, and we're introducing a brand new product. The most accurate scales on the market for weighing sheep.'

'I don't need anything like that to weigh the sheep, I do it myself,' says the farmer.

'How do you mean, sir?'

'You come down to the sheep pen,' replies the farmer, 'and I'll show you.'

So they go down to the sheep pen and the farmer rolls a sheep over, picks it up by the balls with his teeth and says, 'That be six stone ten pounds.'

The salesman is astonished. 'I don't believe it,' he says. 'Are you sure it's right?'

'Check it out for yourself,' says the farmer.

So the rep puts the sheep on his high-tech scales and the farmer has got the weight exactly right. They weigh two or three sheep and the farmer gets every one exactly right.

'Well, that's remarkable,' says the salesman, 'I'm really impressed,' but he's still really determined to make a sale, so he says, 'That's great; it's a tremendous skill – if you can keep it up. But you've got a huge flock of sheep and you won't be around all the time – you could be sick or something like that. How can you weigh them if you're sick or something's happened to you?'

'Oh, my wife can weigh them the same way.'

'I don't believe it! That's ridiculous,' says the salesman.

'Yes she can,' says the farmer. 'I'll prove it to you.' And his little daughter is playing in the barn, so the farmer says, 'Sue, go and ask your mother to come down and show this gentleman how she can weigh sheep.'

'All right, Dad,' she says and she rushes off and comes back a couple of minutes later and says, 'Dad, Mum can't come right now, she's just weighing the postman.'

The scene is an American businesswomen's luncheon club. They've just finished lunch and they're on the coffee and brandies. Suddenly a huge frog leaps on to the end of the table and slowly hops up to the lady president. They are all aghast at this huge, slimy thing. The frog sits on the table and looks up at the lady president and says, 'Ma'am, I've got to tell you something. I'm not really a frog, I'm a Texan oil millionaire and I was turned into a frog by a wicked fairy. I've got to stay like a frog until some lovely woman like you picks me up and kisses me on the lips and tells me that she loves me.'

They're all astonished, but the lady president takes it all calmly. She picks up the frog, puts him into her big handbag and fastens the clasp.

Her friend says, 'Myrtle, what the hell are you doing to that poor guy? Why don't you kiss him and tell him that you love him and turn him back into a Texan oil millionaire?'

She says, 'Enid, I'm not so stupid. I know damn well a talking frog's worth more than any Texan oil millionaire.'

An accountant arrives at the Pearly Gates and says, 'Peter, there's been a terrible mistake, I'm not due up here yet, I'm only 41.'

Peter says, 'Just a minute, I'll look it up in the big book.'

He looks at the accountant and says, 'Sorry, old chap, according to the time you've logged to your clients, you're 125.'

A chartered accountant dies and goes to heaven. St Peter meets him at the Pearly Gates and says, 'I'm sorry old chap, but we've got an overcrowding problem up here in heaven these days and we're only allowing in people who've carried out some act of great courage in their lifetime and, let's face it, as a chartered accountant it's highly unlikely you have ever been called upon to carry out an act of great courage, never mind actually done one.'

So the chartered accountant says, 'Hang about, Peter, in my spare time I'm an international rugby union referee and I was reffing the international game between England and Wales at Cardiff Arms Park. We were into injury time, and Wales were leading by three points. Suddenly the English full-back caught the ball on his 22, ran right the way through the Welsh defence, right down the wing, ducking and weaving and handing them off. He put the ball down by the corner flag over the try line and I awarded a try to England, despite the fact that the Cardiff Arms Park crowd thought the full-back had put his foot into touch two or three times on the way down the wing. I awarded a try to England and England won. At Cardiff Arms Park I think that was an act of great courage.'

Peter says, 'I must agree with you, it certainly was, but I'm afraid that we have been conned a few times by people telling lies about their acts of great courage in the past, and nowadays we have all acts of great courage recorded on the data bank of the heavenly computer. So if you hang on just a minute, I'll recall it from the data bank to check your story.' He presses a few buttons but the screen on the computer comes up blank. 'That's funny, there's no record of it, when did it happen?'

'About four minutes ago.'

A multi-millionaire businessman is sitting in his parked Rolls Royce, smoking a big cigar. He hears a tap on the driver's window, presses the electric button, the window comes down and there's a tramp standing outside.

'Could you give me a quid for a cup of tea and a wad, guv? I haven't eaten or drunk anything for days! I'm starving. I'll give it back to you tomorrow.'

The millionaire says, '"Neither a borrower nor a lender be": William Shakespeare.' He presses the button and up goes the window again.

There's another tap on the window. He brings the window down and there's the tramp again. 'Yes?' he says.

And the tramp says, '"Cunt": D.H. Lawrence.'

Never Work with Animals or Children

Just weave them into your funny stories

There's a very busy road junction controlled by traffic lights. A blind man comes up with a guide dog, and the dog looks at the traffic lights and the traffic and leads the blind man across the road right into the oncoming traffic, and he's almost killed by the cars coming across the junction.

They get to the other side of the road and the blind man stops and tells the dog to sit. He reaches into his pocket, pulls a biscuit out and gives it to the dog and the dog starts to chomp the biscuit. As they are standing there, somebody comes up to him and says, 'What a very kind man you are, sir.'

'What makes you say that?' asks the blind man.

'Well,' says the other man, 'you're blind and you've got your trained blind dog, but that dog almost cost you your life a few minutes ago by leading you across the road against the traffic when he shouldn't have done. You were lucky to get to the other side in one piece. Everybody else would be furious with the dog but not you, you've given it a biscuit, that's wonderful.'

And the blind man says, 'Well, it's not wonderful really, not in that way.'

The other man says, 'Why, how do you mean?'

And the blind man says, 'I'm only giving it a biscuit so I can find out where its arse is, so I can kick it good and hard.'

A chap looks in his back garden one day and sees a gorilla sitting in his apple tree. He's horrified at this 75-stone gorilla calmly resting in his apple tree and he wonders whatever he's going to do about it. Suddenly he remembers that about eight months ago he'd been offered an extension by the Commercial Union on his household policy covering him for the costs of gorilla infestation and he'd accepted and paid the extra premium. So he looks up the policy, gets the telephone number and rings the Commercial Union Gorilla Infestation Department. The guy at the other end says, 'Hello, Gorilla Infestation Department, Craig speaking, how can I help you?'

'Well, I've got this cover with you for Gorilla Infestation and my policy number is RY779375. And I've got a gorilla sitting in my back garden, in the apple tree.'

'No problem, sir,' says Craig calmly. 'I have you on screen. It's Mr Richardson of Clockgate Terrace, Nottingam?'

'That's right.'

'Okay, sir,' says Craig. 'This is quite routine, we deal with three or four of these a week. We'll have somebody with you in about half an hour. Nothing to worry about.'

About half an hour later, sure enough a little van pulls up outside with 'Commercial Union Gorilla Infestation Department' written across one side and 'Don't make a crisis out of a gorilla' on the other. A chap gets out of the van and knocks on the door.

'I believe you have a gorilla problem, Mr Richardson,' says the driver. 'Where is the animal?'

'It's in the back garden, sitting up the apple tree.'

'Well, that's where they normally go. I'll just go get my kit,' and he opens the back of his van and comes back with a huge Irish wolfhound, wearing a muzzle and straining on the leash, and carrying a twelve bore shotgun under his arm.

Calm as you like, he says, 'Take me through to your back garden, sir, and we'll see to it. Nothing to worry about.'

So they go through to the back garden and the CU guy says, 'First of all, I'm going to unmuzzle the dog and let it off the leash, then I'm going to climb up in the apple tree with the gorilla and shake the tree until the gorilla falls out on to the lawn. The dog is trained to go in then and grab the gorilla's balls in his teeth until I can get down from the tree and deal with it. You hold the shotgun.'

'Okay,' says the client, 'but what's the shotgun for?'

The guy replies, 'Sometimes I fall out of the tree first. If I do, you shoot the dog.'

A man goes into a pet shop and says, 'I want a blue and yellow parrot, please.'

So the shop keeper says, 'We've got several parrots, but I'm afraid we haven't got a blue and yellow one. We've got a green one, a brown and grey one and all kinds of other colours, but we haven't got a blue and yellow one. Has it got to be blue and yellow?'

'Yes, I'm afraid it does,' says the customer. 'You see, I'm a perfectionist – everything I do has to be done just right. I'm a member of the local drama society and we're putting on *Treasure Island* and I've got the lead part of Long John Silver. I've read it all up and it says in the book that Long John had a blue and yellow parrot on his shoulder.'

'I see,' says the shop keeper. 'Well, if you can come back in on Thursday, I'll see what I can do.'

'Can't do that,' says the customer, 'that's the day I'm having my leg off.'

Alfred and Henrietta are male and female gorillas in Bristol Zoo, and they fall in love and get into the habit of having sex all the hours of daylight in the outer part of their cage in full view of the visitors. As fast as Alfred has one orgasm, he starts on the next one, and this is ongoing all through the hours of daylight. They only stop now and then to snatch a quick banana to eat.

This attracts the attention and interest of the zoo-going public and they form huge queues to file past Alfred and Henrietta's cage to watch them at it. Then it's featured on TV and people arrive from all over the UK, indeed from all over the world. The queues go right down to the entrance gate, where they're paying £10 a head to come in, and right down the road across the Clifton Suspension Bridge and a mile the other side, rain or shine. The cash flow is astronomical – all this money pouring into the tills.

The zoo director, flushed with the success of this incredible cash flow, decides to extend the zoo and contracts to double the size of the zoo by buying extra land around it. And he also arranges to buy four or five times as many animals, birds and reptiles for the public to see.

Of course, Sod's Law operates, and the day he signs the contracts for the purchase of the land and animals, Alfred dies on the job from a heart attack. What a way to go! Well, they've got a very good insurance broker and they've got 'key man' cover on Alfred, because with his death the cash flow ceases just like that. So they use this key man cover on Alfred to buy a replacement gorilla from London Zoo.

They have him flown down to Bristol and put him in the cage with Henrietta, who totally rejects him. She screams and kicks and bites and struggles and scratches and snarls and they have to take the new male gorilla out because she's going to kill him. Then they buy another male from Glasgow, fly him down and put him in with Henrietta. The same thing happens – total rejection. So there's no enormous cash flow coming in any more and they're going to go bust because of the commitments the zoo director has made.

One morning, desperately worried, the director is strolling past Henrietta's cage and he stops and looks at her. She's slumped in the corner of her cage, grieving for Alfred, totally distraught. As the zoo director watches, he notices that there's a chap sweeping up outside the cage and as this sweeper gets a bit closer to the cage, Henrietta looks up from her grief. If you can imagine a 75-stone female gorilla smiling, she smiles at the sweeper. As the sweeper gets even closer, a seven-foot-long, hairy arm reaches out through the bars of the cage and tries gently to pull the sweeper towards her, but he ducks away. The zoo director sends for the sweeper, who's got to be Irish (otherwise it would spoil the joke), and the zoo director says to him, 'Paddy, you'll be aware of the fact that Alfred's untimely death has caused the zoo some rather serious financial problems in terms of the people coming through the turnstiles.'

'Oh yes, sir, I know that because the people aren't coming in and paying the £10 as they were any more, sir. I realise it must have left you short of cash.'

'Well, actually, it's worse than that, Paddy, it really has caused us some grave financial problems. You'll also have noticed, Paddy, that Henrietta has rejected the two replacement gorillas we bought for her, to take Alfred's place.'

'Yes, sir, I know that, sir,' says Paddy. 'In fact I could have told you that she would. I've been around gorillas for 20 years or more, sir, and they're very loyal, faithful animals. She won't take another gorilla for two or three years yet, no sir, she won't.'

So the zoo director says, 'Paddy, have you noticed that this animal Henrietta seems to look at you rather curiously from time to time.'

'Yes, sir, I have, sir,' says Paddy. 'I have noticed that she looks at me a bit funny. She smiles at me all the time and then she tries to grab me.'

'Yes, I've noticed that, Paddy,' says the director. 'Look, the zoo is in desperate financial trouble and desperate situations demand desperate remedies. You're a big, strapping chap. Would you consider taking Alfred's place? And I'll tell you, Paddy, it'll be a thousand pounds.'

'Well, sir,' says Paddy, 'thank you very much for the suggestion and the generous offer, I do appreciate it, but I'm a good family man and I'd like to talk it over with the wife tonight, if you don't mind, before I say yea or nay.'

'Of course,' says the director, 'that's quite understandable. You do that, Paddy.'

The next morning Paddy comes in and says, 'Sir, I've talked it over with the wife and the answer is yes, subject to three conditions.'

'What are they, Paddy?'

'First of all,' he said, 'there must be no mouth to mouth kissing because her breath smells something terrible.'

'Agreed.'

'Second, sir, any children of the union must be brought up in the Roman Catholic faith.'

'Agreed. What's your third condition?'

'You'll have to give me six months to save up the thousand pounds.'

There were these three cockerels: one was normal, one was dyslexic and the third one was gay. Every morning, the first one would say, 'Cockadoodledoo'.

And the second one would say, 'Doodledoodlecock'.

And the third one would say, 'Any cock'll do.'

A very attractive young woman is walking down the street and passes the window of a pet shop. There's a big sign in the window and it says, 'Clitoris-licking frog available'.

She thinks that'll be something new and walks into the shop. There's a guy behind the counter and she says to him, 'Excuse me, is it true that you have available a clitoris-licking frog?'

And he says, *'Mais certainement, Mademoiselle.'*

Sign in a West Yorkshire Fish and Chip Shop:

'Missing. Grey and black mongrel, one eye, walks with a limp, recently castrated. Name is Lucky.'

There's a baby polar bear and he says to his daddy polar bear, 'What am I, Daddy?'

And Daddy says, 'You're a baby polar bear. You're a beautiful baby polar bear.'

'Are you sure, Daddy?'

'Yes, of course I'm sure. I'm a polar bear, your mummy's a polar bear and you're a beautiful baby polar bear.'

'Daddy are you sure I'm not a brown bear?'

'No, of course you're not.'

'Am I a honey bear?'

'No, you're not, you're a polar bear.'

'Am I a grizzly bear?'

'Of course not, you are a beautiful baby polar bear. Why do you keep asking?'

'Because I'm so fucking cold, Dad.'

The local squire walks into the town brothel – he's Lord Something-or-other and he lives on a huge country estate out in the countryside. He's never visited the brothel before. The madam is absolutely awestruck by the fact that a lord has come to use their services, so she's most ingratiating.

'Oh yes, m'lord,' she says, 'What can I do for you, m'lord?'

'I want a girl,' he says.

'But, of course, your lordship, everyone wants a girl.'

'A very special girl,' he says, 'I want to take her home with me.'

'Well, we don't usually allow our girls to go home with clients, but for you, sir, it's quite different, of course, m'lord. What kind of girl would you like?'

'Oh, a special girl. She's got to be at least seven feet tall, and she must weigh no more than seven stone and she must have very, very long blond hair.'

'Well, I haven't got one just like that, but if you could come back tomorrow I'll have somebody that fits that description waiting for you.'

So he comes back the next night at seven o'clock and there's this girl standing there who's never been a prostitute in her life and she's shaking with terror. But the madam says, 'Here she is, my lord. I've found just the girl for you. She's not quite seven feet tall, but she's six feet ten, and her weight's right, she weighs only six stone actually, and you can see for yourself she has long, long blond hair right down to her bum.'

The squire looks her up and down and says, 'Yes, she'll do. How much?'

'Well, it's normally £50, but if you want to take her home with you it'll be £100.'

'I'll take her,' he says. 'Come on, girl, put your clothes on and get into the car.'

So the girl puts her clothes on, shaking with fear because she's never been in this situation before. They get into his

Rolls and drive without a word into the country and up the three-mile-long drive to the baronial hall.

'Right, come in, come in,' he says, and he ushers her into the library. There's a huge, roaring fire in the fireplace and the lord says, 'Right, get your clothes off.'

The poor girl is absolutely petrified but she takes her clothes off and he says, 'Right, down on your hands and knees in front of the fire.' She's even more petrified at this, but does as she's told and gets down on her hands and knees in front of the fire.

Then he starts to leave the room and he says to her, 'Don't move. I'll be back in a minute.' And he goes to the door and whistles.

Well, the poor girl is beside herself, so when a huge Afghan hound bounds into the room it's all she can do not to pass out.

'Nothing can be worth this,' she's thinking to herself. 'What the hell's going to happen? What am I doing here?'

But the lord is still as matter-of-fact as anything and he takes hold of the dog's collar and drags the dog across to the fireplace and says to him, 'Now look, Arab, that's what you'll look like if you don't eat your Kennomeat.'

There's a dog licking its balls and a fellow says to its owner, 'I wish I could do that.'

And its owner says, 'Give him a biscuit and he'll let you.'

Two drunks are standing in a bar and one says to the other, 'I want to give you a toast.'

'A toast to what?'

'I want to give you a toast. I want us to drink to the health of the male alligator.'

'The male alligator? What on earth do you want to drink to the health of a male alligator for?'

'You ignorant fool, you don't know why we should be so thankful to the male alligator?'

'No, I don't.'

'Well, every six months the female alligator lays 20,000 eggs in the mud at the side of river, but the male alligator comes along and he eats 19,999 of the eggs that the female alligator has laid – that that's why we're drinking a toast to his health. Cheers.'

And his pal says, 'Cheers. Hey, wait a minute. I still don't know why we're drinking a toast to the health of the male alligator.'

And his mate says, 'You ignorant fool, don't you realise, if it wasn't for the male alligator, we'd be up to our necks in bloody alligators.'

A little boy is sent home early from school for wanking in class. He goes home and tells his mother and she sends him up to his bedroom.

When his father comes in, he says, 'Where's little Johnny?'

So the mother says, 'He's been wanking in class and I've sent him up to his bedroom to punish him.'

'Oh, I'll go up and see him.'

He walks into the boy's bedroom and says, 'Johnny, what's this about you wanking in class. You know that'll make you blind, don't you?'

And his son says, 'I'm over here, Dad.'

A class of German children are having an English lesson from a German teacher.

'Today children ve vill have an exercise based on ze English vord, "probably". I would like you each to make a sentence using this English vord. Fritz you vill start.'

Little nine-year-old Fritz stands up and says, 'Last veekend I vas in ze Black Forest viz my familee for a picnic. Ve have a luvly day and I sink ve vill probably go zer again soon.'

'Oh, very good Fritz, zat vas excellent. Hanz, you vill try.'

And ten-year-old Hanz stands up and says, 'Last Tuesday I am valk down ze school corridor and I am passing ze muzic room. I look through ze glass window and zer is my 18-year-old sister vat is having a piano lesson. While I am vatching, she takes her pants down – then ze piano teacher he takes his pants down. I think they is probably going to have a shit in the piano.'

A boy says to his father, 'Daddy, we had some sex education at school today.'

'Oh yes, what was that all about?'

'Well, there were some very, very big words.'

'Like what?'

'Well, one was masturbation.'

'That's a mouthful.'

'No, Dad, that's a blow job. You do masturbation with your hand.'

A man came home to his terraced house which ran back down to the canal. At the end of their back garden was the outside shithouse.

One day, the shithouse was found floating in the canal and the father sent for his 12-year-old son and said, 'Right son, who pushed the shithouse in the canal?'

'I didn't, Father,' said his son and his father said, 'I'll give you one more chance. Who pushed the shithouse in the canal?'

'I didn't, Father.'

So his father said, 'Lad, I want to tell you a little story. It's about George Washington who became the President of the United States of America. George Washington's father came home and found his favourite cherry tree had been cut down. And he said to young George, who was about your age at the time, "George, who cut my cherry tree down?" and he said, "I didn't, Father." So he said, "George, I'll ask you once more, who cut cherry tree down?" and he said, "Dad, I can't tell a lie, I did, I cut the cherry tree down," and his father said, "That was a good lad for telling the truth," and he patted him on the head and gave him a dollar for telling him the truth. Have you got that?'

'Yes, Dad,' the son said.

'Right, now I'll ask you again. Who pushed the shithouse in the canal?'

'I did, Father,' said the son, and his father got hold of him and gave him a damn good hiding and the little boy, tears streaming down his face said, 'What did you do that for?'

'Because you pushed the shithouse in the canal.'

And the boy said, 'But George Washington's father didn't give him a good hiding – he patted George on the head and told him he was a good lad and gave him a dollar for telling the truth!'

He said, 'I know, but George Washington's father wasn't sitting up the cherry tree at the time.'

A ten-year-old girl's periods have started while she's in class at school, so she goes up to the teacher and says, 'Miss, I'm bleeding.'

'Where?' says the teacher.

'Down here,' the girl says and points to her tummy. 'Well,' says the teacher, 'Has your mummy not told you about these things?'

So the girl says, 'No, miss.'

'Well, she will now,' says the teacher. 'There's nothing to worry about. What you'd better do is to go home and talk to your mummy about it and she'll explain everything. I'll get Johnny here to take you home and see you safely across the common.'

So the little girl and Johnny set off across the common and he says,

'Why are you going home?'

And she says, 'Because I've started bleeding.'

He says, 'Where?'

And she says, 'Down here.'

He says, 'Let's have a look,' so she lifts up her skirt and Johnny has a look and says, 'I'm not surprised! Somebody's cut your dick off.'

There's a little boy standing all on his own in Tesco crying his eyes out, so the manager comes to him and says, 'What's the matter, little boy? Why are you crying?'

And the little boy says, 'I've lost my mum.'

'Oh dear!' says the manager. 'Never mind. We'll soon find her. What's she like?'

And the little boy says, 'Sex and bingo.'

A chap's getting ready to go out for the evening to a stag dinner and he's just getting into his dinner jacket and black tie.

His five-year-old son comes into the bedroom and says, 'Oh Dad, you're not going to wear that suit again, you know it always gives you a headache.'

An eight-year-old boy is having his breakfast with his father.

'Dad,' he says, 'how is it that Mum goes out every night at ten o'clock and then comes back at ten o'clock every morning with a lot of money, and wears mink coats and has lovely jewels and everything when you're a bricklayer's labourer?'

And his dad says, 'Shut up and get on with your caviar.'

Love and Marriage

The funny side of relationships

A very attractive girl says to her fiancé, 'Why do you love me, darling?'

'I don't know.'

'Is it because I've got a gorgeous, shapely figure?'

'No.'

'Is it because I have very, very long legs and huge knockers?

'No.'

'Is it because I've got such a pretty face and lovely, lovely skin?'

'No.'

'Is it because of my long blond hair running right down to my waist?

'No.'

'Tell me then, I give in.'

'That's it.'

Dai and Blodwen are going to be married and she says to Dai, 'Look, Dai, I tell you what, when we're married I want you to stop playing this rugby game. It's very dangerous,' she says, 'it could get you hurt and spoil you for life.'

'Good God, Blodwen,' he says, 'I couldn't stop playing rugby, it's half my life. Oh, I couldn't do that.'

'All right,' she says, 'but don't you play next Saturday because we're getting married Wednesday and you could get hurt and spoil the wedding.'

'I can't not play next Saturday, we're playing Pontypridd. The lads would never forgive me.'

She says, 'Well, I tell you what, you just be careful. Don't play your normal rough game, just take it a bit easy. Just remember next Wednesday and all our lovely life together and our honeymoon and everything and the first night and that.'

'Oh, I will,' he says, 'I'll take it easy.'

Of course, the inevitable happens on the Saturday and it's the worst possible thing – somebody kicks him and slices half his dick off. They rush him to the touchline and the doctor's there and he stitches it together again and puts wooden splints down it with bandages round so it will all knit together.

On the wedding night, Dai and Blodwen are in their honeymoon bedroom and she lies there in her nightie and says, 'Now, Dai, I want you to look at this,' and points to her fanny. 'Look at this,' she says, 'it's never been touched by another man, I've been saving it for you all these years.'

Dai says, 'That's nice but look at this,' and points to his dick and says, 'This hasn't even been unpacked yet.'

'I believe you wish to marry my daughter.'

'Yes, sir. I love her very, very much and she's very beautiful and I want to marry her.'

'Are you aware of the fact that she's got acute angina?'

'Yes, sir. She's got lovely tits too, that's why I love her so much.'

A chap says to his friend, 'Do you know, Tony, I'm getting married tomorrow and I'm worried sick about it, because, believe it or not, I've never been with a woman in my life, and I've no idea of what to do when we get into the bedroom together.'

'It's easy,' says his pal, 'it's a piece of cake, nothing to worry about. All you need to do is to go to your bedroom in the honeymoon hotel, take off all your clothes and get your wife to strip off too. Get into bed together, pull the bedclothes up over your bodies, put your left arm round her shoulder, your right hand on her stomach, and say, "I love you, darling". Nature will take care of the rest.'

So the next night after the reception, the couple eventually got to their honeymoon hotel and go to their bedroom. He takes his clothes off, she takes her clothes off and they get into bed together. He pulls the bedclothes over their bodies. He puts his left arm round her shoulder and his right hand on her stomach and he says, 'I love you, darling.'

And she says, 'Lower.'

He says, *(deeper voice)* 'I love you, darling.'

A man sends for his son-in-law and says, 'I've got something very serious to talk to you about.'

'What's that, Dad?' the son-in-law says.

'I'm very concerned about my daughter,' says the man, 'who you married six months ago.'

'What's the matter? What are you concerned about?'

'Well, she's very upset, and she's told me that you've never made love to her since you got married. What's wrong? She's beautiful, she's charming, she loves you – why haven't you made love to her? She's very, very upset.'

'Well, it's because I love her so much that I can't make love to her.'

'What do you mean, you love her so much?' says the father-in-law. 'That should make you want to make love to her all the more.'

'I know, but do you remember that I was married before and my wife died.'

'Yes, I know that, you told us.'

'Well, I never did tell you how my wife died.'

'How did she die?'

'She died because of the size of my prick.'

'The size of your prick? Nobody's got one that size.'

'I have.'

So the father-in-law says, 'I can't believe that. Let's have a look at it.'

So the young man pulls his dick out of his trousers and it's a little thing about the size of a little finger and his father-in-law says, 'That couldn't kill anybody!'

And the son-in-law says, 'It did, it did! It killed my ex-wife. She broke her back snapping at it.'

A bloke is talking to his fiancée. 'Darling, I know I'm not an incredibly wealthy multi-millionaire like Tom Robinson, but I do love you.'

'I love you too, darling.'

'And darling, I know I haven't got a yacht in the South of France like Tom Robinson, but I do love you, darling.'

'I love you too, darling.'

'Sweety, I know that I'm not like Tom Robinson, and I haven't got a 3,000-acre ranch in Mexico, but I do love you, darling.'

'I love you too, darling.'

'Sweetheart, I know that I'm not like Tom Robinson. I haven't got a penthouse flat in New York, but I do love you, darling.'

'I love you too, darling, but tell me more about this Tom Robinson.'

A man is in the waiting room outside the maternity ward and he goes up to one of the other expectant fathers and says, 'Excuse me, I wonder if you could help me.'

'Sure,' replies the guy, 'I will if I can.'

The first one says, 'I've never been a father before, I don't like to ask the doctors or nurses and I understand that this is your fifth, so you'll know. How soon after the birth can I make love to my wife again?'

'It all depends,' says the other guy with a shrug.

'It all depends on what?'

'Is she in a private room or a public ward?'

The Twelve Days of Christmas

December 14th

My Dearest John,

I went to the door today and the postman had for me a partridge in a pear tree! What a delightful, romantic gift. Thank you, darling, for the wonderful thought.

With deep love and affection always,

Your loving Agnes

December 15th

Dearest John,

Today the postman brought your very sweet gift – two turtle doves. I am delighted, they are adorable.

All my love,

Your Agnes

December 16th

Dear John,

Oh! how extravagant you really are. I really must protest – I don't deserve such generosity. Three French hens! I insist you are too kind.

Love,

Agnes

December 17th

Dear John,

Yet another present! This time it's four calling birds. You really are spoiling me.

Love,

Agnes

December 18th

Dearest John,

What a surprise! Today the postman brought me five golden rings, one for every finger. You really are impossible, but I love you. Frankly, all those birds were beginning to get on my nerves with their constant squawking.

Your ever-loving

Agnes

December 19th

Dear John,

When I opened the door this morning, there were actually six bloody great geese laying eggs all over the front doorstep, so we're back with the birds again. Where on earth do you suppose I can keep them all? The neighbours say they can smell them and I can't sleep for the noise. Please stop!

Cordially,

Agnes

December 20th

Dear John,

What is it with these sodding birds? Now I've got seven swans a-swimming! Is this some sort of goddamned joke or what? The house is full of birdshit and the racket ... I'm becoming a nervous wreck. It's not funny. Stop sending bloody birds!

Agnes

December 21st

Okay Buster,

I think I prefer the birds. What the hell am I going to do with eight maids a-milking? If it's not enough with all those birds, now I have eight cows shitting all over the house and mooing all night. Lay off, smart arse.

Agnes

December 22nd

Dear Shithead,

What are you, some kind of nut? Now I have nine pipers playing, and Christ do they play! When they aren't playing their sodding pipes, they're chasing the maids through the cowshit. The cows keep mooing and treading all over the birds and the neighbours are threatening to have me evicted.

You'll get yours.

Agnes

December 23rd

You rotten bastard,

Now we have ten ladies dancing! Although how on earth can one can call those whores 'ladies' is beyond me. They are balling the pipers all night long. The cows can't sleep and have diarrhoea. My living room is a river of shit, and the landlords have just declared the building unfit.

Piss off.

Agnes

December 24th

Listen, Fuckhead,

What with eleven Lords a-leaping – all over the maids, the ladies, and me – we may never walk again! The pipers are fighting the lords for the crumpet and committing buggery with the cows. All the birds are dead and rotting amongst the cowshit after being trampled during the orgy, but not before they had eaten my gold rings.

I hope you're satisfied, you rotten vicious shithouse.

Your sworn enemy,

Agnes

December 25th

Dear Sir,

We are in receipt of your gift of the 25th instant of 12 fiddlers fiddling with themselves, which you sent to our client, Miss Agness Fullbody. We understand this is merely the latest incident in your sustained persecution of our client, who is, at present, residing in the Happy Hours Nursing Home. We are under instructions to charge you with the destruction of our client's home, sanity and genitalia. You are warned not to attempt to contact Miss Fullbody, who has given the Nursing Home staff instructions to shoot you on sight.

A warrant has been issued for your arrest and should be served soon after you receive this letter. Please excuse the cowshit thereupon.

Yours faithfully,

Sue, Grabbit & Runn

Solicitors

PS: Merry Christmas!

A fella's getting dressed in the golf club locker room after a shower, and he's pulling on a pair of camiknickers. His friend says, 'My God, how long have you been wearing those?'

And he says, 'Ever since the wife found a pair in the back of the car.'

A couple who've been married for 50 years are lying in bed and the old lady turns to the husband and says, 'Do you know, George, we have done this so many times, I think we could do it in our sleep. George ... George ... George!'

A man and a woman who have never met before have to share a compartment for two on an American overnight train. She takes the lower berth, and he takes the upper one.

After a while she whispers to him, 'Would you like us to be like husband and wife?'

He thinks he's on to a good thing, so he says, 'Sure.'

So she says, 'Well, darling, get down out of your berth and go and fetch me another blanket.'

And he says, 'If we're behaving like husband and wife, fetch your own fucking blanket.'

A husband comes into the bedroom and sees his wife stroking up and down and round and round her tits.

'What are you doing that for?' he asks.

'I've just read about it in a magazine article,' she says. 'I'm trying to make my tits get bigger.'

'You'd be better getting tissue paper and rubbing it up and down your cleavage.'

'That wouldn't work!'

'It did on your arse.'

A wife says to her husband, 'I've been to the doctor's today, darling, and he says I have the body of an 18-year-old girl.'

And her husband says, 'Did he say anything about your 50-year-old cunt?'

'No, he never mentioned you, darling.'

A couple are sitting in a pub one night and in walk a married couple from Mars. The Martians come across and start having a drink together and chatting, and they tell the couple they're researching life on Earth and their job is to find out about the sex life of earthlings, and they ask the couple if they can go home with them and do a bit of research. So they agree, and it finishes up with the woman going to bed with the Martian husband and the Martian wife going to bed with the man.

The woman and the Martian get undressed and get into bed, and she looks at him and says, 'Goodness gracious, that's a disappointment – the size of your donger, it's very, very small compared with what I'm used to.'

He says, 'Do you want it longer?'

And she says, 'Yes.' So he twiddles his left ear and his penis grows and grows until it's about 10 inches long, and she says, 'That's better! But it's still very thin.' So the Martian twiddles his right ear and his dick gets thicker and thicker until it's a superb specimen.

The next morning the Martian couple have gone and the man and his wife are having breakfast together and talking about their experiences. The man says to his wife, 'How did you get on?'

And she says, 'Oh, I had a wonderful night of passion and love-making. It was fantastic, I've never known anything like it. No disrespect to you, darling, but I've really never known anything like it. How did you get on?'

'Well, it's very funny. I've never known anything like it either. I couldn't understand it. I spent all night with this Martian woman twiddling my ears.'

Mixed feelings are what you have when you watch your mother-in-law drive your new Rolls Royce over a cliff.

Angelo says to Luigi, 'Hey, hey, Luigi, tella me this. Do you lika bigga fatta women witha bigga swingy tits hanging around the waist?'

'Oh no, no, I lika slimma women with a nicea slimma smalla breasts that sticka out all perky.'

'Oh,' says Angelo, '*Bene!* Do you lika women with a lotta blackheads on a the skin, and pockmarks and pimples and things?'

'Oh no, I lika very nicea smootha cleara skin.'

'Do you lika women witha thina greasy, greasy hair, all nasty and smelly?'

'Oh no, Angelo, I lova nice cleana fresha young lady's hair.'

'Thatsa wonderful. Do you lika women witha shorta fatta legs witha dimples on their thighs?'

'No, I lika longa slimma legs.'

'Well, Luigi, tella me something. Whata for you fucka my wife?'

Al Capone finds his girlfriend naked in bed with his best friend, Joe.

'Goddammit,' he says, 'look at you, you bitch, and look at you, Big Joe, get out of bed.' He gets out his automatic and says, 'Joe, I'm going to shoot you. I'm going to show you, you bastard, having my girlfriend. I'm going to shoot you straight in the balls.'

And Joe says, 'Al, Al, give me a chance!'

'Okay,' says Al, 'swing 'em.'

Al Capone's girlfriend has died. He's telling somebody about it and he says to them, 'You know my girlfriend, she died of VD.'

'Al, you don't die of VD these days.'

Al says, 'You do if you give it to me.'

A woman is in bed with a naked, well-built black man, and while they're making love, she hears her husband coming in unexpectedly through the front door.

'For God's sake, quick, quick,' she says, 'get your clothes on!'

'I don't know where they are, I won't have time,' he says.

She's in a panic, but she manages to keep her head. 'Just go and stand in the corner,' she says, 'and stay absolutely stock still. He'll be drunk when he comes in anyway, and I'll pretend you're a statue.'

In comes the husband, drunk out of his brains, and says, 'Hey you, you bitch you, what's that bloody black thing standing in the corner?'

'That's a metal statue,' she says. 'I bought today, isn't it beautiful?'

'It doesn't look like a bloody metal statue to me,' says the husband, 'I don't think that's a statue at all,' and kicks it in the balls – and the black guy says, 'Clang!'

The husband again says, 'I don't think that looks like a statue, it looks funny to me, and he kicks it again in the balls, and the black guy says, 'Clang!!'

'Are you sure that's a metal statue,' says the husband, 'cause it almost looks like it's human,' and he kicks it again in the balls and the black guy says, 'FOR FUCK'S SAKE, CLANG!'

A chap comes rushing home at about six o'clock one evening, goes upstairs and there's his wife lying stark naked on the bed.

'What on earth are you doing?' he says. 'You know we're going out to dinner. We were due out half an hour ago and you're still not dressed or anything. Why aren't you dressed and ready to go?'

And his wife says, 'Oh darling, I've got nothing to wear.'

The husband goes to the wardrobe, slides the door back and starts looking at the dresses along the rail, sliding them along. 'You've got stacks of dresses to wear. You've got the pink one, the blue one, you've got the white and black striped one, you've got the black one, ... hello Fred ..., you've got the purple one ...'

A wife is having breakfast with her husband and she says to him, 'Do you know, darling, I've been wondering, if I died would you marry again?'

The husband thinks for a moment and then says, 'Well, I might do, yes.'

And the wife says, 'If you did marry again, would you live here with your new wife in this house?'

And he says, 'Yes, I think I probably would. It would be silly to go to all the trouble of moving, and it would be expensive to sell this house and get a new one.'

'And would your new wife drive my car?'

And the husband says, 'Well, she might, but she might have one of her own already. If she had one of her own already, I'd sell yours, and if she didn't have one of her own and if she wanted to, I'd let her drive your car, yes.'

'Well, would you let her use my golf clubs?'

'No, definitely not.'

She says, 'Why not?'

He says, 'She's left-handed.'

A very wealthy American came to the UK and advertised for an English rose of a wife who had to be sexually inexperienced. Of course, he had many replies and proceeded to interview 12 of the applicants.

The first one came along and they chatted for a while and he said, 'Well, I've got one more question to ask you,' and he pulled out his prick and said, 'What's that?' and she said, 'That's a prick.' He said, 'Right, that's the end of the interview. I don't wish to know you, you're too experienced. No, forget it, off you go.' So he went through the first 11 applicants and every one said 'It's a prick' and all 11 were dismissed.

So he chatted to the twelfth girl, then he pulled his prick and said, 'What's that?' and she said, 'That's a wee wee.' He said, 'I love you, I'd like to marry you' and in due course they were married and they went on their honeymoon.

They were having dinner together and she said, 'Dear Sam, why did you choose me? I know that you interviewed a lot of other girls and you chose me, why was that?'

He said, 'Because in my advertisement I said that my wife had got to be young and innocent and inexperienced, and I chose you because of the answer you gave to that last question when I showed you my personal parts and you said it was a wee wee.'

She said, 'Well, what's so strange about that?'

'Well,' he said, 'All the other girls said it was a prick.'

'Oh, they must be mad,' she said. 'A prick's a big black thing about 11 inches long, yours is definitely a wee wee.'

Why bother getting married? Why not just meet someone you don't like, and buy them a house!

An 80-year-old woman goes to see the doctor with a distended stomach. The doctor examines her and carries out some urine and blood tests.

'I can't say exactly what it is at the moment,' the doctor says, 'but I've given you all the tests, so if you would like to make an appointment to come back and see me in a week's time, I'll tell you the results and we can decide what we need to do.'

'Thank you, doctor,' says the old woman, and she goes off home.

A week later, she comes back to see the doctor again and she says, 'Well, young man, what is it, why is my stomach so swollen?'

The doctor can hardly believe what he has to tell her but the results are conclusive. 'Madam,' he says. 'You're pregnant.'

'You've got to be joking,' she says. 'I can't be pregnant! I'm 80 years old and my husband is 85. You've got to have made a mistake.'

'It does seem incredible,' says the doctor, 'and I can hardly believe it myself. But we've checked, checked and re-checked – you are definitely pregnant.'

The old lady is ashen-faced. 'That's terrible news,' she says. 'Do you mind if I sit down for a few minutes to recover. And can I use your telephone to ring my husband to tell him?'

'Of course, madam,' says the doctor. 'Please help yourself.'

So she grabs the telephone, dials the number and gets through to her husband and says, 'Hello, do you know what you have gone and done? I'm with the doctor and he's just told me you've gone and got me pregnant.'

And the husband says, 'Yes, who's that speaking?'

Abie dies and is cremated. His wife takes his ashes home afterwards and puts them on the dining room table. She says, 'Abie, I would like to thank you for the money you left me from the insurance policy. I've never had much before, as you know, but now with the insurance money, I've bought diamonds, I've bought a mink coat and I've bought a sports Mercedes. Thank you, darling, for the money, thank you very much, Abie.

'And in your lifetime, darling, you've never taken me on holiday but I've now booked a cruise to the Caribbean and I would like to thank you for leaving me all that money, darling, thank you, thank you.

'And, darling Abie, in your lifetime you never even liked me talking to other men but since you died I've arranged to go out with a toyboy and I'm looking forward to that, darling, and I thank you for leaving me the money and the time to do it, Abie darling, thank you.

'And Abie, you know, I feel that I should do something for you as well. You know that in your lifetime you always wanted me to give you a blow job and I always said no, but now darling, here you are, you can have one.'

And she goes 'Whooooooooosh' and blows all the ashes off the table.

A wife is told by the doctor that she only has 12 hours to live, and she and her husband decide to spend the last evening wining and dining. It's pretty late and they're having a wonderful time.

She says, 'Darling, have another brandy.'

He says, 'No, no, I won't, thank you.'

She says, 'Please have another brandy, we're enjoying ourselves.'

He says, 'No! It's all right for you, you haven't got to get up in the morning.'

This woman's husband goes out drinking every night of the week, comes home very, very late, always drunk, when she's already in bed, then goes to sleep and snores all night. But he always expects her to leave him some sandwiches for him when he gets home.

After years of this kind of ill-treatment she gets very fed up with it and decides she is going to get her own back on him. She decides to leave him cat-food sandwiches so he'll play hell about it. So she opens a can of cat food and makes the sandwiches and leaves them out for him.

The next morning when he comes, down she says, 'Oh, Jim, I'm so sorry, I shouldn't have done that to you last night with those sandwiches.'

'What do you mean?' he says. 'They were fantastic, I loved them. In fact, you can give me those sort of sandwiches every night.' She was so surprised that she told him they were made with cat food.

'I don't mind,' he replied. 'In fact, if you've got any left, I'd like some for my breakfast.'

After that, the man goes completely crazy about cat food. He has it for breakfast, lunch, dinner, and even in sandwiches when he comes in drunk at night. The wife has to buy massive amounts of cat food – she orders 50 tins from the grocer every Friday. The grocer asks her why she wants 50 tins of Kitty Kat because he knows they don't have a cat.

'It's my husband,' she says, 'He's got a madness for it – he eats it all the time.'

'That's weird' replies the grocer. 'But never mind, whatever turns you on.'

This goes on for months and months. Every Friday, in goes the order for 50 tins of cat food plus all the usual groceries. Then, one particular Friday, the order's sent in but there's no cat food on it. The grocer telephones the woman and says, 'Madam, you've made a mistake, you haven't ordered any cat food this week.'

'Oh no,' she says, 'I haven't. Have you heard the news?'

'No,' he says, 'what's that?'

'My husband's dead,' she tells him.

'Dead?' he says. 'But I saw him only a couple of days ago and he looked fine.'

So the wife replies, 'It was an accident.'

'What on earth happened to him?'

'He was sitting on the mantelpiece licking his arse and he fell off and broke his neck.'

A chap is walking down the road with a coffin on his shoulder and he says, 'Where's the wife-swapping party then?'

A chap meets an old pal of his and says, 'You're looking a bit down in the dumps.'

'Yes,' the man replies. 'My second wife has just died.'

'I didn't know your first wife had died,' says his friend. 'What happened to her?'

'She died from eating poisoned mushrooms.'

'That's terrible. What happened to your second wife? '

'Oh, she had a fractured skull.'

'How did that happen?'

'She wouldn't eat her mushrooms.'

A woman goes into a pet shop and says, 'I want a really ferocious pet to deal with my drunken husband and to protect me.'

'What sort of pet do you mean?' asks the assistant.

'Well, have you got some nasty, fierce dog or something like that?' the woman says.

The assistant's face lights up. 'I've got it,' he says. 'I know exactly what you want. You want a Japanese karate bird.'

'A Japanese karate bird, what the hell's that?'

'I'll show you,' says the assistant. 'I've got one over there on that perch.' So he goes over to this perch and unchains this bird that's sitting there. Then he comes back to the counter. He gets two bricks and a thick wooden plank from under the counter, and puts the bricks a little way apart on the counter with the wooden plank on the top and a space in the middle. The woman is watching all this. Then the assistant shouts, 'Japanese karate bird, plank.' The bird comes off the perch and goes flying round the pet shop, comes straight down, lifts up his claw and smashes it into the plank, and the plank falls into two pieces.

The woman is gobsmacked. 'That's fantastic!'

'You ain't seen nothing yet,' says the assistant. 'Watch this!' And he calls out, 'Back on your perch, karate bird,' and it flies back to its perch. Then the assistant puts the two bricks closer together and puts a third brick across the top and says, 'Japanese karate bird, brick.' This time the karate bird comes off the perch, goes swooping round the shop, then comes down and chops with his claw and the brick falls into two pieces.

The woman can't believe it. 'I'll take it!' she says.

'Okay,' says the assistant, 'that'll be £1,000.'

'I don't care how much it is,' says the woman. 'I'll take it. It's just what I need.'

That night she's lying in bed and her husband comes in drunk as usual and says,

'Hello, bitch, how are you, bitch? I'm going to knock the shit out of you in a minute, and what's that bloody stupid thing sitting on that perch?'

Calm as anything, she says, 'That's a Japanese karate bird.'

And he says, 'Japanese karate bird, bollocks.'

Fred goes in to see his doctor who's a big friend of his and he says, 'Mike, Mike, I've got to have your help.'

And the doctor says, 'What can I do for you?'

So Fred says, 'I've got to kill my wife – I can't stand her a second longer! And you've got to help me!'

'But how can I help you?' asks the doctor.

'You've got to give me some poison. I've got to knock her off and finish with her. I can't stand it, she's driving me mad.'

'Fred, don't be stupid,' the doctor says. 'If I give you poison for her, you'll be found out and I'll be found out and we'll both go to prison for life – that's no good.'

'What can I do then?' says Fred. 'I'm desperate, I'm absolutely bloody desperate and we're such old pals, Mike, you've got to help me.'

Mike says to him, 'Well, there's only one way you can do it that's legal.'

'What's that?' asks Fred.

'You can fuck her to death,' replies his friend.

'How do you mean?'

'Well, you've got to be pretty fit,' he says, 'but you are very fit. You've just got to fuck her and fuck her and fuck her until she dies, 'cos if women get too much sex, they die from it – it's a well-known medical fact.'

'I'll do it,' says Fred. 'I'll do it, what's the drill?'

'Just keep at it day and night and never let up – fuck her time and time again every day.'

'How long will it take?'

'About six weeks in total and then she'll die.'

'That's wonderful,' says Fred. 'I'll go and start now.'

Three weeks later, the doctor's driving past his friend's house and he thinks, 'I wonder how Fred's getting on with the plan.' So he turns up the drive, parks his car and his friend is sitting on the veranda in a wheelchair with a blanket over his knees, looking like death. 'How are you?' asks the doctor. 'You don't look too good.'

'I'm all right, Mike,' replies Fred. 'I'm doing what you said, I'm fucking her to death.'

'Well, you look terrible,' replies the doctor.

'No, I'm all right,' insists Fred.

'Where's your wife?' asks his friend.

'Silly bitch,' scoffs Fred. 'She's gone off to play tennis. She doesn't realise she's only got three weeks to live.'

Sex and Other Sports

The Ultimate Source of Fun

A naked woman is lying on the bed with Jean Pierre, the famous French fighter ace. He gets some red wine and pours it on to her breasts and she says, 'Jean Pierre, Jean Pierre, what are you doing?'

He says, 'I am Jean Pierre, the famous French fighter ace, and when I kiss a woman's breasts I like to drink red wine.'

He then gets a bottle of champagne and uncorks it and pours it into her navel and she says, 'Jean Pierre, Jean Pierre, what are you doing?'

He says, 'I am Jean Pierre, the famous French fighter ace, and when I lick a woman's navel I like to drink champagne.'

Then he gets a bottle of brandy and pours it on her fanny and puts a match to it, and she screams, 'Jean Pierre, Jean Pierre, what are you doing, what are you doing?'

He says, 'I am Jean Pierre, the famous French fighter ace, and when I go down, I go down in flames.'

'Get in the back of the car, darling.'

'No, no, no, no.'

'For God's sake, get in the back of the car.'

'No ... I don't want to.'

'Why don't you want to get in the back of the car?'

'I'd rather stay in the front with you, darling.'

A chap sees a sign saying 'Automated brothel' on a building . He thinks to himself, 'I knew they'd invent one of those eventually, I'll give it a try.'

The charge is £10, and he feeds ten £1 coins into a slot machine, the front door swings open and in he walks. He finds himself in a small room. There are two doors out of this room: one is marked 'Brunettes', and the other is marked 'Blonds'. So he decides he fancies a brunette, and he goes through the door marked 'Brunettes', and finds himself in a small room. There's two doors out of the room: one is marked 'Big tits' and the other is marked 'Small tits'. He thinks to himself, 'Well, I like big tits, so I'll go through that door.' So he goes through the door marked 'Big tits' and finds himself in a small room which has two doors out of it. One says 'Tall girls' and the other says 'Short girls'. He thinks to himself, 'I like short brunettes with big tits,' and he goes through the door marked 'Short girls'. He finds himself in another small room and there's two doors out of it, and one says 'Hard cunts' and the other says 'Soft cunts'. He thinks, 'Well, I don't like hard cunts,' so he goes through the door marked 'Soft cunts' and finds himself out on the street again.

Two elderly spinster ladies come into a great deal of money and one of them gets a chunk of her cash and heads off to London to the bright lights and decides that she'll try out this sex thing, which she's never experienced in her life. When she goes back home and gets talking to her sister, she says, 'Oh Edith, it was so fantastic, I can't really describe it properly to you. There I was, lying in bed with this young man and the only way I can describe it is by being poetic and romantic. It was like a flight of wild geese taking off from a distant lake in the mountains in the early morning mist.'

Edith thinks this sounds pretty good so she heads off down to London with some cash and finds the same young gigolo and she's eventually lying in bed with him and she's thinking to herself, 'I can't understand our Judith getting so excited about this nonsense. Flights of wild geese taking off from distant lakes in the mountains early morning mist. Poetic and romantic indeed! She must be going out of her ... oh my goodness, there they go!

Which are the five most important male occupations in women's lives?

A doctor, because he says, 'Lie down.'

A dentist, because he says, 'Open wide.'

A coalman, because he says, 'Front or back, or nutty slack?'

A decorator, because he says, 'How do you like it now it's up?'

And the bank manager, because he says, 'Don't take it out, you might lose interest.'

What's the difference between scuba diving and muff diving?

The view.

The scene is an American household and the lady of the house hears the doorbell ring. She goes to the front door and the milkman is standing there.

'Oh,' she says, 'good morning. I'm glad I just caught you because I've heard that you are retiring today, and I want to say thank you for your 25 years of service delivering our milk – rain or shine. You come on in, milkman, and come on upstairs.' She takes him upstairs, strips off and gets on the bed and they have it off together.

Then she says, 'Now, milkman, you come downstairs because I've got another present for you. Here you are, here's two dollars and thanks again for 25 years of service.'

The milkman says, 'Well thank you, ma'am, that's very good of you. It was great upstairs and two dollars is two dollars, but how the hell did you come to work out that's how you were going to thank me?'

'Well,' the lady says, 'it was my husband Joe's idea.'

He says, 'Your husband? How come?'

'Well,' she says, 'we were having breakfast this morning and I said to Joe, "Do you know, Joe, our milkman's been delivering our milk for 25 years. He's retiring today and I want to thank him so I'm going to give him 50 dollars." And Joe said, "Fuck him! Give him two dollars."'

A man wakes up in bed one morning stark naked, and lying each side of him are two 25-stone, stark-naked, black women, fast asleep. He thinks, 'Oh my God, what was I doing last night when I was pissed? I've got to get out of this.'

So he's crawling over the one on the left-hand side of him and she wakes up and says, 'White man, what's ya doing? What ya think y'all is doing? I is only the bridesmaid.'

The madam of a brothel hears the front doorbell ring, so she goes to the front door, looks around and she can't see anybody there. She's wondering what the hell is going on, when suddenly she hears a voice from the step and there's a chap sitting on the step and he's got no arms and no legs. So she says, 'What do you want?'

'What the hell do you think I want?' he says, 'I want what everybody else comes here for, just the same as everybody else does.'

So the madam replies, 'You're no use to us.'

'Why not?'

And she says, 'You've got no arms and no legs.'

And he says, 'I rang the doorbell, didn't I?'

Mabel and Fred are in the old folks' home and Mabel says to Fred, 'Do you know, Fred, I've got a way of telling exactly how old people are.'

So Fred says, 'How do you do that?'

She says, 'Well, just stand there and I'll show you.'

And she undoes his flies, takes out his prick and strokes and strokes and strokes it until eventually she says, 'You're 79 years, three months, two weeks and two days old.'

And Fred's astonished, and he says, 'How the hell did you know that?'

And Mabel says, 'I asked the matron this morning.'

What's the difference between fear and panic?

Fear is the first time a man realises he can't do it the second time, and panic is the second time he realises he can't do it the first time.

Two nude statues in the park – male and female – standing on plinths quite near to each other and one day a fairy comes up to the male nude statue and says, 'I've been watching you two for the last 80 years while you've been standing here on your plinths. You must really feel extremely frustrated, because you're both naked and you're both beautiful examples of the human form. I can grant a wish every year of my own choice and I've decided this time to grant you two a wish. I hereby grant you the wish that you can take on living form for just half an hour if you would like to – and permission to speak.'

The male statue says, 'Oh fairy, thank you very, very much, you're absolutely right, we've both been so frustrated standing here all these years. Yes, we would like to have a wish and take on human form for half an hour.'

'Right, granted. Don't be late.' And the naked figures leap off the plinths and rush into the rhododendron bushes in the park. There's a hell of a noise coming out, there's rhododendron leaves and dust flying up in the air, screams, squeals and shouts. After 20 minutes, the male's head pokes its way out of the bushes and says, 'How long have we got now?'

'Ten minutes,' says the fairy.

There's about 25 minutes gone with five minutes left and suddenly this male stentorian bellow comes out of the bushes: 'You bloody selfish female bitch! You bloody selfish bitch! Now it's my turn – you hold the pigeon down now while I shit on it.'

A guy has just finished playing tennis and he walks into a pub. He has been serving and he's got two tennis balls in the pocket of his shorts. The publican says to him, 'Good God, what's that down there?'

He says, 'It's tennis balls.'

'I've heard of tennis elbow, but that's ridiculous.'

A sailor and Sharon Stone are shipwrecked together on a desert island, just the two of them. They've been there for six months and have become lovers and they are at it all the time.

One day the sailor says to her, 'Sharon, darling, I want you to do me a big, big favour.'

'I'll do anything for you, darling,' she says, 'I will really.'

'That's great. I've found a piece of wood and I've burned it to make some charcoal, and I want you to draw a little moustache on your upper lip for me.'

'That's odd,' she says, 'but if that's what you want, I'll do it.'

So she gets the charcoal and draws a moustache and turns round and says, 'Hello, Jim, how's that?'

And he says, 'Christ, mate, 'I'm so pleased to see another man! I've been dying to tell someone who I've been fucking for the past six months.'

There's a girl in a field with a bloke and she says to him, 'Darling, take your spectacles off, they are hurting inside my thighs.'

A little bit later she says, 'Darling, put them back on again, you're licking the grass.'

What was 80 years old and smelled of ginger?

Fred Astaire's tool.

A chap says to his girlfriend just before they go to bed, 'How do you like your eggs in the morning?'

And she says, 'Unfertilised.'

A girl walks into the cocktail bar of a West End hotel and says to the barman, 'Good evening, a triple whisky please.'

'Yes, madam.' And she drinks it straight down.

'I'll have another, barman,' she says, and she drinks that straight down.

And so this goes on. She has another, and another, until she has poured 12 triples down her throat in 10 minutes. Then she passes out and falls in a heap on the carpet.

Well, the barman's a bit of an opportunist and he looks round the bar and there's nobody about, so he thinks, 'There's nobody else in the bar, I'm not missing an opportunity like this,' so he drags her behind the bar, rips off her knickers and has his wicked way. Then he realises he'll have other customers any minute, so he rings the manager and asks him to help, as a young lady has collapsed in his bar.

The manager carries the woman into his office, and he's a bit of an opportunist and he looks round and there's nobody about, so he thinks, 'Wow, she's gorgeous! I'm not missing out on this,' and he fucks her as well, while she's still unconscious. Then he decides he should do something about getting her home, so he rings for the hall porter and says, 'Porter, this young lady has collapsed in the bar and we've got to get her home. I've found her card and she lives in a flat in St John's Wood. Would you get a taxi for her, pay for the taxi and have her taken home?'

The hall porter takes the woman, still spark out, into his little lobby and, of course, he can't miss a chance like this with this beautiful woman, so he fucks her as well. Then he rings for the taxi and when the taxi driver arrives, he pays the fare and tells him to take her back to her flat in St John's Wood.

The taxi driver carries her into the back seat of the taxi, and he keeps looking in the mirror at this beautiful woman while he's driving along, and he can't bear to miss out on the opportunity, so he turns into a lay-by and he fucks her on the back seat while she's still unconscious. Then he gets her back to her flat, carries her through the door and says to the concierge, 'Does this young lady live here? She collapsed in the West End.'

'Oh yes,' says the chap, 'she's in flat 92 – I'll see to her.' So the concierge takes her up to her flat and thinks, 'I've been fancying this gorgeous creature for months and months while she's been living here. I can't miss a chance like this,' and he gets her on the bed and he fucks her as well.

The scene is the following evening. It's six o'clock in the same West End bar, and the same beautiful girl walks up to the same barman and says. 'Good evening, barman, a triple gin please.'

And the barman says, 'I thought you drank whisky.'

And the woman says, 'Well, I used to, but I find it makes my fanny very sore.'

There's two old friends talking and one of them says, 'You're looking a bit rough, Fred.'

Fred say, 'Yes, I've got this dreadful headache and I just can't get rid of it.'

'How strange, I've had a really bad headache recently. It went on for months until this doctor told me how to cure it.'

'Oh God, tell me how did you cure it?'

'Well, the doctor told me to go back to my house, rip off my wife's blouse and bra, put my head between her tits and go "Bmrrrrrrm" 20 times, and then make violent love to her. I only had to do that a couple of times and I'm completely cured. You ought to try it!'

'Okay, I will.'

A couple of weeks later the friends met again and the first one says, 'Well, how did you get on with my cure for your headache?'

And Fred replied, 'It worked fine after just three tries. And I like your house too.'

A very sexy, tarty girl is sitting at the end of a bar on a stool. She notices that there are three guys along the other end of the bar, all of whom have stutters, and after a while she decides to go and have a chat. She walks along and says to them, 'Look fellas, I noticed that all you three guys stutter. I like a bit of fun and a laugh or two and I've worked out something we can try if you want to. My suggestion is that if any one of you can say the name of the town where you come from without stuttering, I'll give you a blow job. Would you like to try that?'

'Oh, y-y-y-y-y-yes p-p-p-please,' they all say.

'Fine, well you start.'

The first one concentrates very, very hard and says, 'M-M-M-Manchester.'

'Oh, you've failed, you've failed. Next one, you try.'

He tries. He concentrates very, very hard and says, 'L-L-L-L-Liverpool.'

'No, you're hopeless, absolutely hopeless. Third one, you can try now.'

He concentrates really, really hard and says, 'London.'

'That's it, you've done it, you've done it!' shouts the girl and pulls his zip down and then he says, 'D-D-D-D-Derry.'

A woman gets on to a dreadfully over-crowded bus and has to strap-hang as it bangs it way into town. After a while, she taps on the shoulder of a young man, who is sitting down, and says, 'Don't you stand up for a pregnant woman?'

He says, 'Of course,' and he gets up and she sits down in his seat.

He looks at her and says, 'Excuse me, but how long have you been pregnant?'

And she says, 'About ten minutes.'

It's Christmas Eve, and Santa Claus comes down the chimney into a beautiful 18-year-old girl's room.

She says, 'Oh, Santa, you're so wonderful to come and see me. Give me a kiss.'

'I can't do that,' replies Santa, 'I'm too busy. I've got millions of children to visit tonight.'

'Oh, Santa, I want to kiss you,' she breathes, and she takes off her sweater and her skirt and stands there in her bra and pants.

'No, I'd love to but I've really got to go,' says Santa. 'I haven't got time to kiss you because it would lead to a cuddle and goodness knows what! No, I've got to go.'

'Oh, Santa, I want to kiss you for Christmas,' she sighs, and she takes off her bra and pants and stands there stark naked in front of him.

And Santa looks at her and says, 'Well, I might as well kiss you because I can't get back up the chimney now anyway.'

A stunningly attractive girl with a very, very tight miniskirt is standing in a bus queue waiting for a double decker to arrive. Just before it arrives, she thinks to herself, 'I'll never be able to get up on to the step with this tight, short skirt on,' so she reaches behind her back and fiddles around to find the top of the zip and she loosens the zip a bit on the back of her skirt.

When the bus arrives, the tall, young guy standing behind her presses himself up against her, put his arms right round her and lifts her up on to the platform. Then he gets on the bus himself and keeps his arm around her waist.

So she pulls herself away from him and slaps him round the face. 'What do you think you're doing?' she says to him. 'How dare you do that?'

The poor guy looks astonished. 'Well, frankly, darling,' he says, 'When you put your hand behind your back, groped my dick and undid my flies I thought we were going to be good friends.'

A bloke picks up a prostitute and asks her how much she charges.

'£50,' she says.

So he says, 'I like it rather differently and I'm prepared to pay more.'

'Well, it all depends on what you want,' she says. 'I'll do anything, provided the fee's right.'

'Well,' he says, 'I'd like you to lie down naked and just hold a sheet of plate glass over your face and body. Then I want to shit on the glass – I've got a big piece of it that I use.'

'Well, I've heard them all now,' she says. 'Fair enough, yes, I'll take it on, but it'll be £100.'

'I've got the glass in the car,' he says.

So they go back to her room and she strips off and lies down on the bed naked, holding the plate glass above her body, and he squats over and does one on the plate glass and says, 'That was absolutely wonderful, that was.'

He comes back every Friday night, and keeps doing it every Friday night for six months.

One particular Friday night, she lies down on the bed, puts the glass above her face and her body and he squats down and he's constipated and he just can't hack it. He's straining away there when he hears a funny noise underneath and he looks down and she's crying her eyes out.

'Whatever's the matter?' he says. 'Whatever's the matter with you, what are you crying for?'

She says, 'You know what's the matter – you don't love me any more.'

Two builders are working overtime on a site and they stroll to the window to look out into the street below while they have a cigarette break, and see that there are two dogs there having it off together. One of the builders says to the other, 'God, look at that, I've never tried that, I wonder what it's like?'

'Have you never tried it? It's great, it's tremendous. You ought to try it with the wife tonight.'

'I'll do that, I'll do it this very night.'

Next morning his pal says to him, 'Well, did you try it last night with the wife doggy fashion?'

'Yes,' says the guy, sounding a bit dubious.

'What was it like?'

'Well, it was okay once we got down to it, but there was one problem.'

'What was that?'

'I had a hell of a job getting her out into the street.'

A policeman finds a man in the woods, stark naked, tied with his hands round a tree, with his face pressed against the bark.

'What on earth happened to you?' he asks the man.

'I was driving along in my car and this chap pulled me up and asked for a lift, and then he said he just wanted to go for a wee and I did too, so we came into the woods here, and he held me up with a gun, told me to take off all my clothes, stole all my money, stole my car, but the worst of the lot is that he tied me up like this with my face to the tree and then had his evil way with me! Please help me.'

The police constable pulls his zip down slowly, walks slowly towards him, and says, 'This just isn't your day, is it?'

Adam is in the Garden of Eden and God calls to see him.

'Good morning, Adam,' says God.

And Adam says, 'Good morning, God, nice to see you, thanks for popping in. Any news?'

'Well, Adam, I do have some news actually. I've decided that you must be lonely on Earth here all by yourself.'

'Oh, not really, God. I've got plenty to occupy myself and you pop in every so often to have a chat. No, I'm okay really. Why, what did you have in mind?'

'Well, bearing in mind that I thought you were lonely, I've created someone to keep you company.'

'What do you mean, God? Who is he, what's he like?'

'Well, actually, Adam, it's a woman.'

'What's a woman, God?'

'Well, she's very similar to you but with some physiological and psychological differences, but she's different enough to make life interesting for you in so many ways, so I've bought her along to meet you.'

'Well, where is she, God?'

'Well, she's over there in those bushes. She wants to meet you without me being there at the time.'

'What's her name, God?'

'Her name's Eve.'

'Well, what happens now, God?'

'I want you to go into those bushes and talk to her and come back and tell me what you think.' So Adam trots off into the bushes. He's away about 20 minutes and when he comes back, God says to him, 'What did you make of that, Adam?'

'Not much, God. She doesn't seem to know much, she's not switched on about what's going on in the world, but she seemed to talk a lot about things that don't really matter. But I suppose it's okay, yeah, in small doses. Is that it?'

'Well, no, there's a bit more to it than that, I want you to go into the bushes now, put your arms around her and kiss her.'

'What's kiss, God?'

'Well, it's a way of – well, you put your mouth against hers – it'll come naturally to you once you start.'

'It sounds very insanitary to me! I could catch the flu or all kinds of things off her. But you reckon it's all right?'

'Yes, Adam, I think you'll find it's quite pleasant.'

'It sounds crazy to me, but if you say so, you're the boss, I'll go and try it.'

He disappears into the bushes and comes back 15 minutes later, looking a bit flushed with his eyes sparkling a bit and God says, 'Well, did you enjoy that?'

'Well, I rather did, God. I didn't expect to, but I must say I did enjoy that. It was a remarkable feeling and I also got the feeling that wasn't the end of it – there's something more to it than just kissing her.'

'Well, there is, Adam, I want you to go and copulate with her now.'

'What's copulating, God?'

So God describes copulation to him and Adam laughs his socks off, and says, 'God, you've got to be joking. That's ridiculous, put that in ... you're pulling my leg now, aren't you, God?'

And God says, 'No, I'm deadly serious, that's what you do. That's copulation.'

'Well, you're the boss, God. I'll go and try if you say so. You were right about the kissing, so you might be right about the copulation.'

So off he goes into the woods again and he comes rushing back three minutes later and says, 'God, what's a headache?'

It's Grand Central Station, New York and there's a long queue at one of the ticket booths, mostly because the young girl issuing the tickets is wearing a very low-cut dress and every time she leans forward to operate the machine, there's a good view down the front of her dress, displaying her cleavage. The queue moves very slowly and there's a very impatient older chap at the back of the queue.

When he gets to the front of the queue, he says, 'I think this is disgusting. I've been standing here for 20 minutes trying to get my ticket and because I've waited so long, I've missed my train, and it's all because of your boobs. This whole country, the whole of America, is obsessed with women's boobs – they can't think of anything else. It's on the hoardings, it's in the newspapers, it's in magazines – all the time boobs, boobs, boobs.'

And she says, 'Can I help you, sir?'

And he says, 'Oh, yes. Give me a picket to Titsville.'

A businessman travels to Tokyo and is duly entertained by his Japanese hosts, who supply him with a beautiful Japanese geisha girl to spend the night with him.

They're lying in bed together and starting to have sex when suddenly she starts shouting at the top of her voice, 'Pusharda, pusharda, pusharda, pusharda!' so he does his best and he tries to go a bit harder and exhausts himself.

The next morning, he's out playing golf with his host. It's a beautiful golf course and they have a caddie to look after them. The man has just put his ball down on the tee and he's about to hit it with his wood when the caddie shouts, 'Pusharda, pusharda!'

And the businessman turns to his host and says, 'Why's he shouting "pusharda"?'

And the host says, 'It means "wrong hole".'

A chap picks up a woman for sex and they drive out into the country and go into a very dark lane. They get into the back seat and he makes love to her.

She says, 'Do it again,' and he does it again. And she says, 'Do it again,' and he does it again, with an effort. And she says, 'Do it again,' and he says 'I'm sorry, I can't handle this. In fact I need some fresh air.'

He gets out and walks up the lane, has a cigarette and meets a chap walking his dog. He has a brainwave and says to this chap, 'Do you like women and sex and that sort of stuff?'

And the chap says, 'Yes, I love it, why?'

'I've got an insatiable woman in my car. She's so horny, I can't cope with her. I've done it to her three times already and she wants me to do it again, and I really can't. Would you like to take over?'

And the chap says, 'Yes, you take my dog for a walk and I'll take over the woman in your car.' So he gets into the car and he's hammering away at this woman, having a wonderful time, and there's a tap on the window and a torch shines in through the window of the darkened car. He rolls down the window and it's a policeman.

The policeman says, 'What's going on here, sir?'

And the man says, 'It's all right officer, this is my wife.'

And the policeman says, 'I'm sorry, sir, I didn't know.'

'Neither did I till you shone your torch into the car.'

A lesbian goes to the doctor with an itchy fanny and the doctor says, 'Drop your knickers,' and examines her and says, 'Well, it looks very clean.'

The lesbian says, 'It should be, I have a woman in three times a week.'

The scene is the Thames Embankment and a young tramp is just settling down on a bench, pulling the newspapers over himself to have a good night's sleep, when a beautiful Rolls Royce pulls up by the kerb. From the driving seat of this Rolls Royce there emerges a gorgeous 22-year-old blond girl with a wonderful figure, a beautiful mink coat and all the trimmings.

She says to this tramp, 'Look, I've just spotted you lying there with newspapers over you on this very cold night and I want to do something for you. Get into my car and I'll take you home with me and you can spend the night in my house and have some comfort for a change. It might change your luck altogether.'

The tramp can't believe his luck, so he gets into the Rolls Royce and they drive back to Sloane Square. She takes him to her house, the butler comes to the door and she says, 'James, I want you to take this young man to the guest room, run a bath for him and lend him a razor and trim his hair a bit. There's a suit in the wardrobe which I'm sure will fit him. Just clean him up generally, get him dressed and bring him downstairs. He's going to have dinner with me in an hour's time.'

The butler says, 'Very well, madam,' and takes the tramp up to this sumptuous room, runs a bath for him in the luxury bathroom, gives him shaving tackle and fresh towels, trims his hair and shows him where everything is. When he comes out of the bathroom, there's the suit laid out on the bed with a clean shirt and shoes, the whole works.

An hour later, the tramp goes downstairs to the dining room. The table is laid for two people, with candles in the centre and all the silver and cut glass and the finest china. They have a most fantastic meal served by the butler, with lots of wine, followed by some superb vintage brandy. Then the young lady takes him up to his room and says, 'Well, there you are, have a good night's sleep and I'll see you in the morning.'

The tramp undresses and gets into this huge feather bed. And he's just beginning to doze off when suddenly there's a little tap at the door and in comes the girl in a totally transparent, gauzy negligée. She comes over to the bed in a waft of erotic, expensive perfume and presses her face against his ear and whispers, 'I've been thinking. I've given you a new start in life tonight. You've been bathed and you've had a meal and some wine, it seems a pity that the rest of it isn't happening, and I think I should get into bed with you and just have a snuggle with you. And she gets into bed, and says, 'Move over a bit nearer.'

And he moves over a bit, and she says, 'Move over a bit more.'

And he moves over a bit more and falls into the Thames.

A clerk in Australia House says to an Englishman, 'Why are you emigrating?'

And the man replies, 'It's this homosexuality.'

'How do you mean, homosexuality?'

'Well, 25 years ago, homosexuality was illegal. Then 15 years ago they made it legal between consenting adults in private. Ten years ago, they made it totally legal. I want to get out of here before they make it compulsory.'

Two chaps are in a public lavatory in London. One of them says to the other, 'Would you like to come to a party tonight mate? Lots of sex, perversion, drink, drugs – you name it!'

'Yes, who'll be there?'

'You and me.'

There's a bunch of prostitutes and a customer goes up to one of them and says, 'You look lovely. How much do you charge?'

She says, '£350.'

'What? £350! That's an enormous amount, how come you're so expensive?'

And the prostitute says, 'Well, I've got a first class honours degree in prostitution at Southampton University.'

'Oh, how fascinating, how very fascinating. I would have loved to have gone with you but I'm afraid I can't afford £350. Can you recommend one of the other girls?'

The prostitute says, 'Yes, try that redhead over there, she's much cheaper.'

So he goes across to the redhead and says, 'How much do you charge?'

And she says, '£10.'

'Oh,' he says 'That's fine, that's better. That girl across there quoted me £350 and it's all because she's got an honours degree in prostitution from Southampton University. Shame though, 'cause I'd loved to have tried somebody who'd really qualified in the art.'

And the redhead says, 'Well, I went to university, but I just didn't get the degree.'

'Why not?' he asks.

'Because I failed the oral.'

A couple were arrested for having sexual intercourse on the grass on the side of Beechers Brook at Aintree. They were charged by the police with gross indecency, and taken to court.

When the case came up they asked for six other fences to be taken into consideration.

A chap's sitting at the bar of a pub and he notices that amongst the people in the pub there's one very attractive young girl sitting on her own at a table near the bar. After a while, he plucks up courage and walks across to her and says, 'Excuse me, miss, but I notice that you are sitting on your own and I'm on my own. I wondered if you would mind if I join you and buy you a drink and we can have a chat together.'

She looks at him and shouts at the top of her voice, 'I know what you're after, you're after my body! You want to take me to bed and make love to me – I've met your kind before.' This is all at the top of her voice and all the people in the bar turn round and look at them.

The chap is utterly embarrassed and says, 'I'm sorry, I'm sorry,' and goes back to his seat at the bar. He's cringing with embarrassment and sits there thinking, 'Oh my God, how terrible. What must these people think? Everyone keeps looking at me.'

About an hour goes by and the attractive girl suddenly gets up, walks across to him and quietly says to him, 'I'm terribly sorry, I must explain to you what's going on and why I said those things to you. I'm a student of psychology at university and I'm doing a thesis on embarrassment. I was testing to see how you would react to what I said. I wanted to see how you wold react in those circumstances when I shouted out all those things to you.'

And this fella looks at her and shouts at the top of his voice, '*How* much? – a *hundred quid*?'

There are four kinds of rugby – Rugby Union, Rugby League, Rugby Junction and Rug be buggered, let's go to bed and have it in comfort.

A gay says to his partner, 'Do you know, Lawrence, I think our sex life is getting a bit boring because we just do it the same and the same and the same. Heterosexuals have all kinds of different ways of having sex, they do, all kinds of different ways, and I think we ought to try something different.'

So his pal says, 'Well, which way could we try it differently?'

'Well, if I blindfolded you and I stuck different things up your bum, you'd have to guess what they were, and we'd have a bit of fun and a laugh doing that, then you could do the same, the other way round, to me. Would you like to play this game?'

And his pal says, 'Yes, that'll be fun.'

'Right, here's the blindfold, drop your trousers.' Lawrence drops his trousers and his pal says, 'Bend over,' and he gets one of those big, black ebony rulers off his desk and stuffs it up his friend's bum, and he works it up and down a bit and wiggles it about a bit and says, 'Right, Lawrence, what do you think that is?'

'Oh, I don't know, move it up and down a bit more. It's nice! Move it up and down a bit more.' So he moves it up and down a bit more and says, 'What is it then, Lawrence?'

And his pal says, 'I've got it now, it's that big black ebony ruler off your desk.'

'That's right,' says his friend, 'that's right! Now, number two coming, I want you to guess this one,' and he does it himself with his prick and says, 'What's that?'

And his pal says, 'I'd know that anywhere, that's you, that's you sweetheart, that's lovely, oh, do it some more, I love it.'

Then he takes a ... a ... a ... *(look as if you have forgotten the word)* 'one of those long, green vegetables ... *(one of your listeners will almost certainly say 'cucumber', then you say to him)* I see you've played it!

My wife said to me, 'George, it's about time you learned to play golf.' You know golf – that's the game where you chase a ball all over the country when you're too old to chase women.

So, I went to see Jones and asked him if he'd teach me how to play.

'Sure,' he said. 'You've got some balls, haven't you?'

'Yes,' I said, 'But sometimes on cold mornings they're kinda hard to find.'

'Bring 'em to the clubhouse tomorrow and we'll tee off,' he said.

'What's tee off?' I asked.

'It's a golf term,' he said, 'and we have to tee off in front of the clubhouse.'

'Not for me! You can tee off there if you want to, but I'll tee off behind the barn somewhere.'

'No, no! A tee is a small hard thing about the size of your little finger.'

'Yeah, I got one of those,' I said.

'Well, you stick it in the ground and you put your balls on top of it.'

'Do you play golf sitting down, then?' I asked. 'I always thought you stood up and walked around.'

'You do. You're standing up when you put your balls on the tee.'

Well, folks, I thought that was stretching things a bit too far and I said so, but he ignored it. He said, 'You've got a bag, haven't you?'

'Sure,' I said.

'Your balls are in it, aren't they?' he said.

'Of course,' I told him.

'Well, can't you open the bag and take one out?'

I told him I supposed I could, but I was damned if I was going to.

He asked me if I didn't have a zip fastener on my bag but I told him no, I was the old-fashioned type.

Then he asked me if I knew how to hold my club. Well, after 50 years I should have some idea and I told him so.

He said, 'Take your club in both hands.' Folks, I knew right then he didn't know what he was talking about. Then he said, 'You swing it over your shoulder.'

'No, no, that's not me you're talking about,' I said, 'that's my brother.' He asked me how I held my club. Without thinking, I said I held it in two fingers. He said that wasn't right and he'd show me how. He couldn't catch me there because I didn't put in four years in the navy for nothing. He said, 'You hit the ball with your club and it will soar and soar.' I said I could well imagine. Then he said, 'When you are on the green ...'

'What's the green?' I asked.

'That's where the hole is,' he said. 'Sure you're not colour blind?' I asked. He said he wasn't. Then he said, 'You take your putter' – that's the smallest club made, that's what I've got, a putter – 'and with it you put your ball in the hole.'

'You mean the putter,' I said.

He said, 'No, the ball. The hole isn't big enough for the ball and the putter too.' Well, I've seen holes big enough for a horse and wagon.

Then he said, 'After you make the first hole, you go on to the next seventeen.' He wasn't talking to me. After two holes I'm shot to hell. 'You mean,' he said, 'you can't make eighteen holes in one day?'

'Hell, no,' I said, 'It takes me eighteen days to make one hole. Besides, how would I know when I'm in the eighteenth hole?

And he said, 'The flag'll go up.'

That would be just my luck.

On the Bench

Laughs at the expense of the legal profession

A judge is sitting on the bench looking down at the body of the court.

'I am quite disgusted with the crime of which you have been found guilty,' he says to the defendant. 'To imagine that you were prepared to indulge in sexual relations with a wire-haired fox terrier in broad daylight in the high street of this town in front of women and young children is beyond my belief. To think you could copulate with a dog in a public place! I just don't know what punishment fits the crime.'

And someone from the body of the court shouts, 'Give him the cat.'

An important case is being heard in the law courts and one of the witnesses in the morning says to the judge, 'Your Honour, may I be excused from being in court this afternoon because my wife is in hospital and is about to conceive.'

The judge looks at him and says, 'I think you are mistaken. Surely what you mean to say is that your wife is about to give birth to a child. But whichever is the case, you should certainly be there.'

The scene is a divorce court and the judge is trying a very turgid case. He comes wearily into his chambers after the case, takes off his wig and slings it in the corner, then he turns to his clerk and says, 'Oh God, Jones, what a terrible case. I never slept with my wife before we were married, did you?'

And Jones says, 'I can't remember, sir, what was her maiden name?'

The judge says to the defendant in court, 'Prisoner at the bar, you are accused in this court today on two very serious charges. The first one is of indecent assault on a 17-year-old girl. What do you plead to this charge: guilty or not guilty?'

The defendant has a fit of coughing and with a very hoarse voice says, 'Not guilty, m'lud.'

'Very well,' says the judge. 'The second charge on which you are arraigned is one of indecent exposure in a public place. What do you plead to this charge: guilty or not guilty?'

Again the prisoner has a fit of coughing and spluttering and in a very hoarse voice says, 'Not guilty, m'lud.'

The judge is quite a thoughtful old sort, so he says to the prisoner, 'Would you like to suck a Fisherman's Friend?'

And the prisoner says, 'I think I'm in enough trouble already, your Honour.'

The judge says to the defendant, 'Prisoner at the bar, please tell the court exactly what happened on the day in question.'

'Well, your Honour, I'm walking along the fucking road and sees this fucking piece of fucking stuff on the other fucking side of the fucking street walking along the fucking pavement. I fucking catches her fucking eye, and she fucking catches mine, and I fucking wink and fucking smile at her. She fucking winks and fucking smiles back, and fucking beckons to me to come across the fucking road. So I crosses the fucking road, through the fucking traffic, and fucking chat her fucking up, your Honour, and she fucking well invites me fucking back to her fucking flat. We walk along the fucking pavement, arm in fucking arm, back to her fucking front fucking door, go up the fucking stairs to her fucking flat, in through the fucking door of her fucking flat and into her fucking bedroom. She takes my fucking clothes off and I take her fucking clothes off and we gets on the fucking bed together stark fucking naked.'

There's a long pause until eventually the judge says, 'What happened then?'

'Intimacy took place, your Honour.'

A couple go to a divorce lawyer and he asks them how old they are.

The husband says, 'I'm 95 and the wife's 92.'

'Why have you waited so long for a divorce?'

'We've been waiting for the children to die.'

An Irish stipendiary magistrate is on the circuit and he's in a particularly unpleasant Irish town, which he hates to death; he's always glad when he gets out of it again. This time, however, he suddenly goes down with a rather severe dose of the flu. He sends for the clerk of the court and says, 'Paddy, I've got the flu, I can't take the court tomorrow, but I hate coming here. I'm sorry, I know you live here, but I hate your town, I hate coming here. Look, there's only some very insignificant cases on tomorrow for me to take. What I'd like you to do is nip out into the street and the first reasonable-looking chap you find, put my wig on him and my glasses, and get him to sit in for me on the bench. Nobody knows me very well here and they'll think it's me, and you can tell him what to do. Then I shan't have to come back here till I'm due again, instead of coming back here next week.'

So the clerk agrees to do this and goes out into the street and gets hold of the first reasonable-looking guy he can find and asks him if he'll be prepared to stand in on those lines, and the chap agrees. But what the clerk doesn't realise is that he has got hold of the local town drunk who's already halfway down his first bottle of Irish whiskey.

In due course, the drunks sits up on the bench with the stipendiary magistrate's wig and glasses and so on, and the first case comes up. The clerk reads out: Micky O'Reilly, you are charged in this court with driving your motor car along the main street of the town at 45 miles an hour when the speed limit is 30. How do you plead to this charge?'

And the accused shrugs his shoulders and says, 'Guilty, your Honour.'

The clerk to the court turns to the stipendiary magistrate and nods to him. The dummy stipendiary magistrate, drunk as hell, puts the black cap on his wig and says, 'Prisoner at the bar, you have been found guilty on your own admission of the heinous crime of driving your car down the main street of this town at 45 miles an hour in a 30-mile-an-hour limit. The sentence of this court is that you will be taken from here to a place of legal execution and there hanged by the neck until you are dead, and may the Lord have mercy on your soul.'

The clerk to the court whispers furiously to him, 'A £10 fine, a £10 fine!'

And the dummy magistrate says, 'And you'll be fined £10 as well.'

Wilber is charged with rape and the principal witness is Lulubell. The judge says to her, 'Lulubell, gal, you just tell the court exactly what happened on this terrible evening.'

'Sure will, your Honour. I was sitting in the kitchen in my rocking chair reading my library book, and that Wilber he doggone busted into my kitchen, he knocked me on the kitchen floor and he raped me. Then he raped the dog and he raped the cat, then he went upstairs and raped my daddy and my mammy and then he came down again and raped my grandpappy and my grandmammy. He raped my two brothers and my three sisters, he raped my uncle, he raped my auntie. He came back into the kitchen again, your Honour, and then he raped me for the second time.'

'Was that it Lulubell?'

'No, your Honour, that wasn't the end of it. He picked my glasses up off the floor, fixed them on his John Thomas, looked down at it and he said, 'Now, Wilber, you have a good look round boy, and see if you's missed anything.'

The Church and Other Services

Vicars, policemen, pilots and soldiers

(Sung in a chanting voice as in a church service.)

'I am the vicar of the parish. I take the morning and evening services on Sundays and I do the principal weddings, baptisms and funerals and I get £150 a week for tha-a-at.'

'I am the curate of this parish. I do all the dirty work that the vicar doesn't want to do himself and I do the nasty bits of visiting and I take the services and the weddings and the baptisms and the funerals when he's too pissed to do it himself, and I get £100 a week for tha-a-at.'

'I am the organist of this parish. I play the organ for the Sunday morning and evening services, the principal weddings, baptisms and funerals and I get £25 a week for tha-a-at ... but I also play the organ in the local nightclub on Thursdays, Fridays and Saturdays and I get £500 a week for that and *(stamp the feet in time)* there's no business like show business.'

Two nuns were in the bath together and one of them says, 'Where's the soap?'

And the other one looks around bit and says, 'Yes, it does, doesn't it.'

A vicar marries a prostitute. The night before the wedding, the prostitute goes to see her mother and says, 'Mummy, darling, I'm very, very worried about marrying the vicar tomorrow.'

Mummy says, 'Why, darling? Because I know you love him.'

'I love him to death, but the trouble is that as soon as he sees the size of my fanny tomorrow night he's bound to realise I've been on the game for years and he thinks I've never been with a man – that I'm a virgin. How in hell's name can I cope with it? And Mummy, darling, I know you were on the game before you married Daddy, so how did you handle this problem?'

Mummy says, 'Oh, darling, it was very difficult for me in my day, and I won't bore you with how I did it, but it's so easy for you now. You must buy one of these second-skin body stockings and what you do is wear it when you go to bed. Don't tell the vicar. He'll never realise what you're wearing – let him try and fight his way through and just play it by ear when he's having difficulty.'

So the vicar and the prostitute get married and, in bed in their honeymoon room that night, he starts trying to make love to her and he's getting rejected by this second-skin body stocking. He's getting nowhere at all. After letting him try for about 10 minutes, the prostitute says to her husband, 'Darling, you're having some trouble aren't you?'

'Oh yes, sweetheart, I am.'

'Well, Mummy told me that we'd probably have a problem because I've never been with a man before, so she's given me some very special ointment to rub into my whatsit. Because of the possible difficulties, I've got a pot of the ointment in the bathroom. Shall I go and put some on?'

'Oh, yes please, honey, please, please.'

So she nips across to the bathroom, takes off the second-skin body stocking, gets back in bed and they have the most wonderful sex all night long.

The next morning the vicar's out cutting the lawn and a bee comes buzzing round, gets on his neck and stings him. The vicar reaches round and manages to grab the bee and pulls it off his neck. He says, 'You naughty little animal you, imagine you stinging me, a man of the Church, when I'm on my honeymoon and I'm so terribly, terribly happy. There's no need for you to sting me and you deserve punishing for that. But I don't quite know which punishment fits the bill – whether I should pull your legs off so you can't walk, or pull your wings off so you can't fly. But on reflection, what I'm going to do is I'm going to get some of my mother-in-law's ointment and I'm going to stuff this lawnmower up your arse.

A nun is driving along when she's pulled up by a police car with the blue lights flashing. The police constable stops his car behind hers and walks back to her car, gets in the passenger seat with her and says, 'Sister Mary, this is really absolutely too much! This is the twelfth time I've pulled you up for speeding and I've let you off each time because of your cloth. Really, it's not good enough! You're going to kill yourself one of these days with speeding. But I'm warning you again, you really must take it easier because you'll kill yourself and other people and we'd hate to lose you.'

Then he pulls his zip down and Sister Mary says, 'Oh no, not the breathalyser again.'

A gay guy is talking to a recruiting sergeant and the sergeant points straight at him and says, 'Your king wants you.'

'Oo, what an honour,' says the gay.

'Not for that, you fool, he wants you for the Army.'

'Oo, what a contract!'

A little boy sees a priest and he says to him, 'Hey mister, why have you got your collar on back to front?'

So the priest explains, 'I'm a father.'

The boy looks puzzles and says, 'You're not my father.'

'No, you don't understand, sonny, I'm a father to thousands.'

'It strikes me, then, you ought to wear your trousers back to front.'

An 82-year-old man stands in the middle of the town crying his eyes out and a policeman goes up to him and says, 'Whatever's the matter, Grandad? What are you crying for?'

'It's terrible, terrible.' sobs the old man. 'I'm 82, married to a lovely 21-year-old girl. We make love every night, she cooks like an angel and cleans the house till it shines like a new pin.'

Puzzled, the policeman says, 'Well, what on earth are you crying for?'

And the man replies, 'I can't remember where I live.'

An old colonel is being interviewed in a sex survey, and this young lady says to him, 'Tell me, colonel, when was the last time you had sex?'

So the colonel says, 'Now, let me think. It was 1926.'

She says, 'Wow, that seems a long time ago.'

'Oh I don't know,' says the colonel, pointing to his watch. 'It's only 2028 now.'

A reporter says to an RAF pilot, 'What was it like being a dambuster?'

The RAF pilot says, 'It was like making love in a canoe.'

'Making love in a canoe, how come?'

'Fucking close to the water!'

A chap goes for a medical for the armed forces. He's very fit but he has two parallel scars running down each cheek about six inches apart. The examining doctor says to him,

'You are perfectly fit and certainly okay for service in the army, but I'm most intrigued by those scars running down your cheeks.'

The man gets very angry and says, 'Mind your own bloody business. You're here to check me out for the army. These scars don't affect my fitness for the army, they're nothing to do with you, so mind your own bloody business.'

The examining doctor is a bit taken aback and tries to apologise. 'I'm terribly sorry,' he says, 'I didn't mean to be personal and it's obviously not a subject I should have brought up. But I was just interested in them from a medical point of view because I've never seen anything quite like them before. I would certainly appreciate it if you would help my research and any information would be entirely confidential.'

So the chap is mollified and he shrugs and says, 'Well, all right, you've been very polite about asking, but it's something I do feel quite touchy about. The fact is I was breast-fed until I was seven, and the scars were a result of getting my lunch through the school railings.'

A Luftwaffe bomber pilot is shot down over England during the Battle of Britain and his leg is injured. He's taken to a prisoner of war camp in Northern Ireland and put into the camp hospital.

One day, the doctor comes up to him and says, 'I'm terribly sorry, Fritz, I have very bad news for you. You have gangrene in your foot and we are going to have to amputate it.'

Fritz says, 'Well, it's all part of my duty to my beloved Fatherland, but I would ask you one favour. When you have amputated my foot, will you please arrange for it to be taken on the next bombing raid over Berlin and dropped over my beloved Fatherland. I'll know then that at least a part of my body will be buried back where it belongs.'

The doctor says, 'Sure, Fritz, we'll do that for you with pleasure.'

Two weeks later, the doctor says, 'Fritz, I have more bad news for you,' and Fritz says, 'What is that?'

And the doctor says, 'I'm afraid that we haven't stopped the gangrene and we are going to have to amputate your leg up to the knee.'

'Well, again I would ask you this favour, that when you have a bombing raid over Germany you will drop that part of my leg over Germany so that I will know that part of me is buried back in my beloved Fatherland.'

'Okay,' says the doctor, 'We'll do that.'

Two weeks later the doctor comes to Fritz again and says, 'I've got some more bad news for you. I'm afraid we haven't stopped the gangrene and we're going to have to take off your leg up to the top of your thigh.'

And Fritz says, 'Well, again, I would ask you to ...' and the doctor says, 'I'm sorry, Fritz, I know what you're going to ask and I've been talking to the camp commandant about it, and he won't let us do it.'

'Why not?' says Fritz.

'He says he thinks you're trying to escape.'

An old colonel is giving a lecture on his expedition to Kilimanjaro and how he shot the sabre-toothed tiger.

'We trekked through the foothills for a couple of days and then started climbing the lower slopes. We identified the spoor of the sabre-toothed tiger and started to follow it. We climbed and climbed, following the spoor. We knew we were getting closer and closer because the spoor was becoming fresher and fresher. As we got halfway up, in quite a lot of bush, we came into a clearing and there sitting in a tree on the other side of the clearing was the sabre-toothed tiger of Kilimanjaro. I lifted my trusty rifle and prepared to shoot it, but the sabre-toothed tiger leapt out of the tree and came bounding towards me. *Ohhhhhhhhhhh*, I wet myself.'

One of the audience said, 'Well, that's the sort of thing that I can understand with a large ferocious animal like that leaping at you.'

'No, not then, you fool, just now, when I went *Ohhhhhhhhhhh*.'

There's an Englishman ...

And several others from around the world

An Englishman, a Scotsman and a Irishman are working on a North Sea oil rig and they're absolutely starved of sex – they are desperate. So they decide to send off for one of these very sophisticated blow-up plastic dolly birds.

When it arrives, they draw lots as to who'll roger it first and the Englishman wins and gets the doll for the first night.

In the morning, the Scotsman and the Irishman are all eager and curious and keep asking him what it was like.

'It was bloody fantastic,' says the Englishman. 'Do you know, it was so realistic that I kept thinking I was back home in bed with the wife.'

The Scotsman gets it the next night, so the following morning, the others ask him what it was like.

'Och, it was incredible! I had two or three orgasms with the thing, I wouldn't have believed it was possible. Incredible value, wonderful value.'

So the Irishman gets it the next night and the following morning, they want to know how he got on.

'Well, you know, the bloody thing,' he says, 'I'm getting a bit worked up, so I gave it a love bite and you know what happened then? It farted twice, flew around the room three times and jumped out of the window.'

The *Titanic* is sinking. An Englishman, an American and a Frenchman are standing on the deck. The Englishman says, 'Women and children first.'

The American says, 'Fuck the women.'

And the Frenchman says, 'Ave ve got ze time?'

An Irishman, a Welshman and an Arab are sitting having a drink together and chatting. The Irishman says, 'Begorrah, I'm such a lucky guy, I've got ten sons and my wife's pregnant. One more son and I've got enough to start a football team.'

The Welshman says, 'I'm even luckier than you are, Pat. I've got 14 sons and my wife's pregnant. One more son and I've got enough for a Rugby Union team.'

The Arab says, 'You two are very, very lucky guys. I'm not lucky, because I've got 17 wives, but I've got no children at all.'

And the Irishman says to him, 'Don't be so stupid, you're very lucky. One more wife and you've got a golf course.'

You know what Russian roulette is – well, this is African roulette.

A missionary is captured by natives in Africa and they sit him on a swivel chair, surrounded by 12 naked, voluptuous native women. They swing the swivel chair round and round and round until he stops facing one particular naked woman. She walks forward and gives him a blow job.

So what makes that African roulette, you may ask?

One of them is a cannibal.

An Englishman, a Frenchman and an Italian are arguing about who is the most sexual woman who ever lived. The Englishman says, 'It's got to be Greta Garbo, the old film star. She had this air of mystery and incredible sexual allure. Yes, I'll definitely go for Greta Garbo.'

The Frenchman says, '*Messieurs*, I think I must go for Marilyn Monroe. She was the most incredible sexual woman who ever, ever lived.'

And the Italian says, 'I do not agree with you. I think Sara Pippalini was the most sexy.'

The other two say, 'Sara who?'

And the Italian says, 'Sara Pippalini.'

The Englishman says, 'I've never heard of her. How do you make that out?'

The Italian says, 'I have read the newspaper report about this Sara Pippalini. She was laid by 300 men in 60 days.'

So the other two say, 'What are you talking about, we've never heard of anything like this.'

'I have the newspaper cutting from the *Daily Telegraph*,' insists the Italian, 'and I show you,' and he takes this newspaper cutting out of his wallet.

The Englishman reads it and shakes about with laughter and says, 'Oh, you Italian clot. This is the Sahara Pipeline.'

A Native American says to the tribal elder, 'How come my name? How come I get my name?'

'Aah,' says the wise, old Indian, 'Name always given after first thing squaw see after papoose arrive when she open flap of tepee – like Sitting Bull, Raging River, Blue Sky. But why do you ask, Two Dogs Fucking?'

A Polish squadron leader is speaking to the girls at the top public school, Roedean, at their annual prize-giving, about his experiences in the Battle of Britain.

'One day in September 1940, I am flying my Spitfire at 8,000 feet over London and suddenly I look in ze rear view mirror and zer is 12 Fokkers flying straight at me, firing zer machine guns. I look to ze starboard side and zer is eight Fokkers flying straight at me, firing zer machine guns. I look to ze port side and zer is six Fokkers flying straight at me, firing zer machine guns.'

These being the girls of Roedean School, a little titter runs round the audience. The Headmistress leaps to her feet and says, 'Oh girls, I should tell you that when the squadron leader talks of Fokkers, he's speaking of a famous German fighter aircraft in the Second World War.'

The squadron leader leapt to his feet and said, 'Yes, but these Fokkers was flying Messerschmidts.'

The scene is an Australian wedding reception, and all the guests have arrived and are chatting and enjoying a glass of wine. After about half an hour, the bride's father stands on a chair and shouts, 'Ladies and gentlemen, I am very sorry to tell you that the wedding reception is now cancelled, for two reasons. One, we've run out of beer and two, the best man's raped the bride.'

The guests are just finishing their drinks and getting ready to leave when suddenly the bride's father stands on the chair again and says, 'Ladies and gentlemen, I am pleased to tell you that the whole thing is now on again for two reasons. One, we've located some more beer and two, the best man's apologised.'

A fella goes to Paris on holiday and stays at a backstreet Parisian hotel. He can't speak any French and none of the residents or staff he meets can speak any English. When he comes down to breakfast the first morning, the restaurant is crowded and he has to sit at a table with a Frenchman. As he sits down the Frenchman says, 'Bon appétit, Monsieur,' and the Englishman thinks he's telling him his name, so he says, 'Robinson.'

The next morning he comes down to breakfast and sits with the same Frenchman again and once more the Frenchman says, 'Bon appétit,' and the Englishman still thinks it's his name and he says, 'Robinson.'

Later that afternoon he's talking to the hotel manager, who speaks some English. He says to the hotel manager, 'You know, I find you Frenchmen are extraordinarily polite.'

'What makes you think that, Monsieur?'

He says, 'Well, I've been down to breakfast two mornings recently and sat with the same Frenchman and each morning he's introduced himself and told me his name and said, 'Bon appétit'.

'Oh, Monsieur,' says the manager, 'I'm sorry but he is not telling you his name, he is wishing you bon appétit – it means have an enjoyable meal. He hopes that you will enjoy your food.'

'Oh, good Lord,' says the Englishman, 'that's terrible. I've been telling him my name – Robinson – he must think I'm mad. I must put that right tomorrow.'

The next morning he sits with the same Frenchman again and as they sit down, before the Frenchman can say anything, the Englishman says, 'Bon appétit' and the Frenchman says, 'Robinson.'

The scene is mid-Atlantic during the Second World War, and there's a German U-boat on the surface belting shells and torpedoes into an unprotected British convoy. The ships are going down right, left and centre. Suddenly, the look-out on the conning tower of the U-boat shouts, *'Achtung, achtung!* Zer is a British destroyer flotilla approaching.'

So the captain orders, 'Dive, dive, dive!' and they all pour down the conning tower, pull the hatch down, 'clang', and screw it down tight. They all scramble down below and the captain says, 'Flood ze tanks and dive, dive, dive.'

The U-boat sinks to the bottom, 200 feet down. The captain picks up the tannoy and says to the crew, 'All must now be quiet. No engine running, no speaking, no noises of any kind, ozzerwise ze Asdics in ze destroyer flotilla will hear us and depth charge us, and kill us all. ALL QUIET.'

The whole ship goes quiet except for something going, 'ching, ching, ching, ching, ching, ching, ching, ching, ching.' The captain turns to his first officer and whispers, 'Vat is zat going "ching, ching, ching"?'

His officer says, 'I do not know, *Herr Kapitan.'*

So the captain says, 'Go immediately *und* find out vat ziss "ching, ching, ching" is and stop it immediately, ozzerwise ve vill all be dead men.'

'Jawohl, Herr Kapitan.' Off he goes and five minutes later the noise has stopped and the first officer returns.

The captain says to the first officer, 'You found out vat vas ziss "ching, ching, ching"?'

'Jawohl, Herr Kapitan.'

'Vat vas it?'

The first officer says, 'It vas the second engineering officer vat vas playing vis himself in ze toilets.'

'So you stopped him?'

'No,' he says, 'I took his cufflinks off.'

There's a Lufthansa 747 in mid-Atlantic, and the captain comes on the tannoy and says, '*Achtung, achtung*, this is your captain speaking. Please I would like all ze passengers to look out ze port side where you vill see zat ze outer port engine has fallen off into ze sea. Ziss is an unfortunate accident but it should not affect our flying and ve can maintain height okay vizout ziss engine.

'Now please look to ze starboard side where you vill see ze inner starboard engine is a little bit on fire; some flames and smoke are coming from it. Ve have operated ze automatic fire extinguisher and vill soon have ziss fire under control. Ziss aircraft can maintain height on two engines only, so zer is nothing to vorry about.

'Now please look rear to ze port side and you will see zat half ze tail plane is missing. Ziss is because we hit a large goose just after take-off from Heathrow, but as you can tell, ve are already halfvay across ze Atlantic and zere is nothing to worry about. Ziss aircraft is not affected at all by ziss mishap.

'Now look forward to ze air conditioning grills at tze front of ze cabin. You vill see zat smoke is coming from these. Ziss is some kind of electronic short circuit but nothing to vorry about – ze flight engineer is trying to locate it and put it right.

'Finally, please for me vould you to look to ze sea which is 35,000 feet belows. In ze sea you vill see a little yellow spot. Ziss is a liferaft and ziss is vere I am speaking to you from ...'

An Australian is on a beach with a girl and he says, 'Hey, Sheila, do you want to fuck?'

She says, 'No.'

'Well, would you mind lying still while I do?'

A Frenchman is talking to his mate about the impossibility of women, and he says, 'One day I go down to my favourite café and I have a little drink of cognac. I don't know what the cognac do to me, but it makes me think of my Louise, and I go to my Louise's flat and I love her once, I love her twice, I love her three times. Then I go back to the café and I have another little drink of cognac. I don't know what the cognac do to me, but it makes me think of my beautiful Louise, and I go to my Louise's flat and I love her once, I love her twice and I love her three times. Then I go back to the café and have another little drink of cognac, and I don't know what the cognac it do to me, but it makes me think of my beautiful Louise. So I go to my Louise's flat and I love her once, I love her twice and I love her three times.' *(You can have Henri going back to see Louise as many times as you like, and it's suggested you not only tell this in a French accent, but also try to sound a little more drunk as you progress.)*

'Then I go back to the café and have another little drink of cognac, and I don't know what the cognac it do to me, but it makes me think of my beautiful Louise. So I get a taxi and go to Louise's flat and I love her once, twice and three times. Then I go back to the café and have another drink of cognac. I don't know what the cognac it do to me, but it makes me think of my beautiful Louise. They put me in the ambulance, take me to Louise's flat, carry me in on the stretcher. I stagger to my feet – I am very weak – and I go into Louise's flat and I walk towards her, one, two, three, four but, *sacré bleu*, I am too weak, and I fall flat on my face at her feet.

Louise look down at me and she say to me, 'Henri, are you going out with another woman?'

An Englishman goes to the Emigration Department at Australia House. The clerk behind the desk says to him, 'What can I do for you, cobber?'

He says, 'I want to emigrate to Australia.'

The clerk says, 'Do you have a criminal record?'

And the English guy says, 'Why, do you still need one?'

This is a telephone conversation that takes place in California.

Ring, ring, ring ring, ring.

'Buenos dias. Is that Maria the maid?'

'Si, señor.'

'Is my wife there?'

'No, señor.'

'Don't lie to me – she is there, isn't she?'

'Si, señor.'

'Is she alone?'

'Si, señor.'

'Don't lie to me – is she alone?'

'No, señor.'

'Is she with a man?'

'No, señor.'

'Don't lie to me – is she with a man?'

'Si, señor.'

'Are they in the bedroom?'

'No, señor.'

'Don't lie to me – are they in the bedroom?'

'Si, señor.'

'Maria, get my gun out of the dining room and go and shoot them both'

'Si, señor.'

Footsteps receding into the distance are heard and then there's two loud bangs and the footsteps come back again to the phone and she says, *'Señor,* what shall I do with the bodies?'

'Maria, throw them in the swimming pool.'

'Señor, we do not have a swimming pool.'

Pause, then, 'Is that Beverley Hills 493 0727?'

An Irishman is sitting in a bar on his own and he sees a gorgeous girl sitting further along the bar. He walks up to her and says, 'Let me buy you a drink, honey. You're very beautiful and I'm alone and you're alone and we can have a lot of fun.'

'No,' she says, 'I'm not interested.'

'Why not?'

'Because I'm a lesbian.'

'What's a lesbian?'

She says, 'Well, let me explain. You see that gorgeous girl sitting at that table over there, wearing the low-cut blouse?'

'Yes,' he says.

'Well, I'd like to go across there and slip my hand down her blouse and fondle her breasts, then I'd like to reach down and slide my hand up her thighs and rub all round her fanny. Then I'd like to kiss her passionately and put my arms round her and hug her and kiss her, and that's because I'm a lesbian.'

And the Irishman says, 'Do you know, I think I'm a lesbian as well.'

The Last Word

Word play and rhymes

This is the story of Rindercella and her Sugly Isters.

Rinders and her sugly isters lived in a marge lansion. Rinders worked very hard, frubbing scloors, weaning clindows, emptying poss pits and shivelling shut. By the end of the day she was nucking fackered. Her sugly isters were fight cucking runts. They did no wucking ferk and had no wucking forries. They were right bugly astards. One was called Mary Hinge and the other was called Betty Swollocks and they were always pucking fissed.

The two sugly isters had tickets to go to the ball. Rindercella was ducking fisgusted when the cotton runts wouldn't let her go.

Buttons worked with Rinders. He was gifted with nuge hackers, a brig pick and a shairy hithole. He was a candy runt and liked Rinders to give him a wood gank. He was always diving into Rinders' hubic pairs and asking for a joe blob.

Suddenly, there was such a bucking fang and a Gairy Fodmother appeared. Her real name was Sherry Tighthouse, and she was a light rucking fesbian with a carge lairy hunt and tairy hits. She changed a pumpkin and six mite whice into a hucking cuge farriage with six dandy ronkeys with buge hollocks.

Rinders was amazed. 'Miste all crucking fighty,' she said. The Gairy Fodmother said Rinders must be back at midnight or there would be a cucking falamity.

At the ball, Rinders was dancing with the pransome hince. The band was gucking food, but foo nucking toisy. It was that drucking fummer – what a rucking facket. The pianist was hucking fopeless. When the leader blew his trucking

121

fumpet he was bucking frilliant but he was a big-headed banky wastard, and they wished he would stick his trumpet up his ucking farsehole.

Suddenly the clock struck twelve. Rinders pucking fanicked and ran out of the ballroom, tripping tarse over its and dropping her slass glipper.

The next day, the pransome hince came knocking at Rinders' door. The sugly isters let him in and Betty Swollocks lifted her leg and let off a fig bart.

'Who's fust jarted?' said the pransome hince.

'Blame that forrible hucker over there,' said Buttons. The shell of smit was tucking ferrible. The pransome hince tried the slass glipper on the sugly isters without success. They had horrible fetty sweet and fetty swannies. Suddenly Mary Hinge in a tucking femper gave the pransome hince a nick in the kackers. This was not difficult as he had bucking fuge halls and a hig bard on.

The pransome hince tried Rinders and the flipper sitted pucking ferfectly. 'Well, puck my siles,' said the hince. 'Suck your own,' said Buttons.

Soon Rinders and the pransome hince were married. He ended his days in lucking fuxury – she ended hers with a follen swanny.

And they all hived lappily aver efter.

(And if it's Christmas time, wish everyone a 'Crappy Histmas.')

If a brassiere is an upper-topper-flopper-stopper,

and a jock strap is a lower-decker-knacker-checker,

and a toilet roll is a super-dooper-paper-scraper,

what is a punch-drunk Japanese boxer with a father suffering from dysentery?

He's a scrap-happy-Jappy-with-a-crap-happy-pappy.

Allegedly by AP Herbert

The portion of a woman which appeals to man's depravity

Is constructed with considerable care,

And what appears to us to be a simple little cavity

Is really an elaborate affair.

So scientific doctors who have studied the phenomenon,

When visited by apprehensive dames,

Have made a list of everything in the feminine abdomenon

And given them delightful Latin names.

The vulva, the vagina, the jolly old perineum,

The clitoris, and God knows what besides.

With a host of other gadgets you would love if you could see 'em

And the hymen – which is sometimes found in brides!

So isn't it a pity that when we fellows chatter

Of the mysteries to which I have referred

We should use for such a delicate and complicated matter

Such a very short and unattractive word.

Index